THE LIFE CYCLE SERIES

Adolescence

generation under pressure

John Conger

HARPER & ROW, PUBLISHERS

London   New York   Philadelphia
Hagerstown   San Francisco   Sydney

This book was devised and produced
by Multimedia Publications Inc

General Editor: *Dr. Leonard Kristal*
Prod Mgr/Art Dir/Design: *Bob Vari*
Picture Researcher: *Judy Kristal*

First published in Holland 1979 by
Multimedia Publications Inc

Published in Great Britain by
Harper & Row Ltd, 28 Tavistock Street London WC2E 7PN

British Library Cataloguing in Publication Data
Conger, John
    Adolescence: generation under pressure
    References pg. 120–123
    Includes index
ISBN 00631 81002   cased
       00631 80995   paper

Colour origination: United Artists Ltd, Israel
Typeset by CCC and printed by William Clowes & Sons Limited
Beccles and London

Contents

I

A time for becoming

'Standing in front of the mirror,
I'm wondering what that person is all about.'
                                        Tony Hall, aged 16.

Adolescence, more than any other age, holds us in its spell. Over the centuries, no period in life has been more celebrated—and condemned—by poets, philosophers and politicians. It is easy to recognise some contemporary views in those irritably thrown out by Aristotle 23 centuries ago: the young, he said, 'are passionate, irascible, and apt to be carried away by their impulses, especially sexual impulses ... in regard to which they exercise no self-restraint. They are changeful too, and fickle in their desires, which are as transitory as they are vehement ... If the young commit a fault, it is always on the side of excess and exaggeration ... They carry everything too far, whether it be their love or hatred or anything else. They regard themselves as omniscient ...'[1]

Not that there is no more favourable view of youth, for which poets have had memorably kind words, and on which old men look back with regret and a sense of loss. Even that stern genius, Joseph Conrad, had his nostalgic memories of lost vigour and intensity: 'Only a moment; a moment of strength, of romance, of glamour—of youth! ... A flick of sunshine upon a strange shore, the time to remember, the time for a sigh, and—goodbye!—Night—Goodbye ...!'[2] Somewhere between the excess and the ecstasy lies the real human experience, that same experience that Samuel Butler, in *The Way of All Flesh*, characterised as 'like a spring, an over-praised season—delightful if it happens to be a favoured one, but in practice very rarely favoured and more remarkable, as a general rule, for biting east winds than genial breezes'.[3] Yes, it is not all fun.

But what lies behind this long-standing fascination with adolescence? In part it is a recognition that young people are our links to the future, our guarantee of continuity for our species, our own vicarious triumph over death and failure. But there is also a more personal side to our preoccupation with youth. For most of us, adolescence is remembered as the time

'Passionate . . . and apt to
be carried away by their
impulses' said Aristotle
of adolescents: no less
true now than
in ancient Greece.

when our identities began to crystallise, when our potentialities were at their height; when, whatever the pains, we lived most intensely. And if we are old and unsatisfied, perhaps some of us also resent the adolescents about us as the enviably uncaring inheritors enjoying 'what we never had'. Nevertheless, we are looking at *ourselves*—mirrors of our own desires, hopes, fears and satisfactions.

A time of change

Adolescence can be a time of irrepressible joy and seemingly inconsolable sadness and loss; of gregariousness and loneliness; of altruism and self-centredness; of insatiable curiosity and boredom; of confidence and self-doubt. But above all adolescence is a period of rapid change—physical, sexual and intellectual changes within the adolescent, environmental changes in the nature of the external demands placed by society on its developing members.

Time of change, time of contrasts—even the adolescent may not know whether to opt for wholesome convention or vulgar affront.

At no other time, from the age of two onwards, does the individual undergo as many changes as during the period surrounding puberty. Small wonder that so many adolescents, faced with an ever-changing physical image in the mirror, conscious of new—and sometimes strange—feelings and thoughts, ask themselves 'what that person is all about'.

Developmental 'tasks' of adolescence

The changes in puberty give to adolescence a certain universality as a separate stage of development. But the developmental 'tasks' young people are expected to master may vary—sometimes widely— from one society to another, both in kind and degree of difficulty.

The strong urge towards sexual exploration may be masked under boisterous horseplay.

In preliterate societies, the tasks to be mastered may be relatively simple and few in number, and represent only a gradual emergence from earlier stages of development. Among the Mountain Arapesh people of New Guinea, for example, there is a slow transition from a high degree of dependence and indulgent care in infancy and early childhood to increasing independence and responsibility as the child grows older.[4] There is no discernible 'spurt' during puberty or adolescence. Unlike youth in many Western countries, there is no societal or familial expectation that a boy will leave home and obtain an unfamiliar job, if necessary in a strange community.

The Arapesh girl, by the time she reaches adolescence, has already been chosen as a wife by her future husband's parents, and has gradually learned to assume the daily responsibilities of a household. Neither boys nor girls are pushed into sexual relationships and marriage. When these events do occur in the natural course of time, they are with a partner each has known, cared for and adjusted to over a long period.

Fitting into an adult world: the young are equally apt for disciplined violence ...

In contemporary industrialised societies such as our own, however, the adolescent is expected to master developmental tasks far more numerous and more complex; and there is a much more rapid shift from childhood dependence, with its relative lack of responsibility. In the years between puberty and nominal adulthood, the contemporary adolescent may be expected to achieve independence from his or her parents, to establish new kinds of social and working relationships with peers of both sexes and with adults, and to adjust to increasing sexual maturity and changing roles (including a consideration of the possibilities and demands of marriage and parenthood, or alternative relationships). In addition, he or she will be under pressure to decide on personal educational and vocational goals, and to prepare for the responsibilities of active citizenship.

In the process of meeting these challenges, the adolescent must also gradually develop a 'philosophy of life'—a view of the world and a set of guiding moral beliefs and standards that, however simple and basic, are 'non-negotiable'. Finally, the young person must develop a sense of his or her own identity.

'Who do you think you are?'

W. H. Hudson, author of *Green Mansions*, spent an idyllic childhood in the back country of Argentina—a time to be lived close to nature, rather than thought about. But, as he writes in his autobiography, there came the critical moment of realisation that such times come to an end.

Fifteen years old! This was indeed the most memorable day of my life, for on that evening I began to think about myself, and my thoughts were strange and unhappy thoughts to me—what I was, what I was in the world for, what I wanted, what destiny was going to make of me!... It was the first time such questions had come to me, and I was startled at them. It was as though I had only just become conscious; I doubt that I had ever been fully conscious before...[5]

As Hudson's experience illustrates, a central task of adolescence is that of finding some kind of workable answer to the question, 'How do I fit into the world?'—or, simply, 'Who am I?' This has been the key question of much western philosophy, at least since the 'Age of Reason', and some of our greatest works of imaginative literature have revolved around this puzzle of personal identity. Yet only in recent decades has it become the subject of systematic psychological investigation, largely through the work of Erik Erikson, a gifted writer as well as a psychologist and psychoanalyst.

In Erikson's view, an indispensable task of adolescence is the development of a *sense of one's own identity*: 'Before the adolescent can successfully abandon the security of childhood dependence on others, he must have some idea of who he is, where he is going, and what the possibilities are of getting there'.[6]

... or for peaceful socialising games.

I doubt whether anyone can have survived the past couple of decades, except possibly on a desert island, without hearing the term 'adolescent identity crisis'. I became aware that this term had successfully invaded popular thinking some 20 years ago when I asked an adolescent boy what he felt was bothering him, only to be told: 'I guess I'm having an identity crisis.' So widespread has this term become that Erikson himself was recently led to wonder if so many young people would be manifesting 'identity crises' if they didn't think they were supposed to.

Nevertheless, the concept of identity is a crucial one in understanding adolescent development, and it is important to know exactly what we mean by it. It is also vital to correct a number of misconceptions, including the notion that the problem of identity development either begins or ends in adolescence.

The adolescent, or adult, with a strong sense of identity sees himself or herself as a distinct individual. Indeed, the very word 'individual' as a synonym for 'person' implies a universal need to perceive oneself as somehow separate from others, no matter how much one may share motives, values and interests with them. Closely related is the need for self-consistency—for a feeling of wholeness. When we speak of the 'integrity' of the self, we imply both a separateness from others and the unity of the self—a workable integration of needs, motives, and patterns of response. Finally, a clear sense of identity calls for a self-perceived stability of the self over time; that is, the need to perceive the person that one is today as similar to, and having consistent links with, the person one was yesterday, and will be tomorrow.

Exploring possible roles, searching for identity, begin even before adolescence sets in.

But adolescents need time to integrate the rapid changes of body and mind into a slowly emerging sense of unitary identity. I recently asked a young girl why she had three distinctly different handwriting styles, and she replied: 'How can I have just one style till I know who I am?'

Many adolescents have similar feelings. Not only do they find themselves playing roles that shift from one situation or one time to another, and worry about which, if any, is the '*real me*', but they also self-consciously try out different roles in the hope of finding one that seems to fit.

But to say that the problem of identity is a central one in adolescence does not mean that the task of identity formation either begins or ends there. The beginnings of ultimate identity are shaped early in life. The process starts in infancy and

The expectations of adults may lay the foundations of a lifelong style and foreclose the choice of individual identity.

continues through all the partial identifications that a growing child forms with parents, peers, siblings and non-familial adults, well into mature life.

Nor is the individual's sense of identity necessarily fully developed in adolescence. Unfortunately, it happens too often that a young person's struggle to achieve a rich, full and unique identity is 'prematurely foreclosed', to use Erikson's term, as soon as he or she gets out of school and begins to work or gets married. Instead of finding themselves, they become like everybody else.

There are, however, those who become more genuinely individual and more sure of themselves in relation to the world as they grow older. This is obvious in the cases of such famous people as Einstein, Eleanor Roosevelt and Gandhi. But it is equally true of many people of whom nobody but their immediate family and friends has ever heard.[7] Such people are not hard to recognise, but may be hard to accommodate in rigidly-ordered

11

Even within the rigid conventions of a boarding school, adolescents will find a way to individualise themselves.

societies: wide latitude is allowed in universities for the development and display of strongly individual ways of life—but an idiosyncratic identity in, say, a barrack-room or boarding school may attract hatred or even persecution.

Variations in identity formation

The process of identity formation can be relatively simple or complex, brief or prolonged, rewarding or agonising, successful or unsuccessful, depending on many factors. In contemporary society the possibilities are broad and there are great opportunities for personal growth and development. However, the very multiplicity of potential choices can be confusing and there is little unanimity in our society regarding appropriate values and life-styles—the kinds of jobs that are most worthwhile, acceptable sexual values and behaviour, the role of the family, or appropriate roles for women or men. The young person is increasingly left to his or her own resources.

Those who succeed may develop richer, more interesting identities. But there are also likely to be more casualties, more victims of what Erikson calls *identity confusion*. Unless the adolescent can somehow achieve a clear sense of personal identity, he or she will become like a rudderless ship, changing course with each passing wave.

Parents can play a vital role in aiding or hindering the development of a strong sense of identity. Those with well-defined identities of their own, who can serve as sound role models for their children, will make the task a lot easier.

So far I have been talking about factors promoting or hindering the development of a positive identity. Unfortunately, however, the only protection that some adolescents have against identity confusion is development of a *negative* identity. Rather than risk failure by continuing to fight against all the social forces that conspire to keep them 'nothing', some may adopt a negative, deviant identity, and take pride in achieving a totally consistent nothingness. This can be seen in the case of some delinquents and 'social dropouts'.

The attempts of those less fortunately placed to 'make their own mark' may end in disaster or disgrace.

To a significant degree, we tend to live up to others' expectations of us. If those expectations are for a strong, successful sense of identity and for personal and moral integrity, they are likely to develop. But if the expectation is for identity confusion or defeat, or for unreliability and moral opportunism, those, too, are likely to develop. The striking thing to me about so many of the obviously bright, personable, attractive young people who played their junior parts in the Watergate tragedy was the extent to which they seemed programmed. Their identities seemed imposed on them by others over the years, rather than developed organically from forces within themselves. This may have had much to do with their vulnerability to the pressures put on them to conform to the prevailing morality during adolescence.

Sexual identity

An important part of one's overall identity is one's sexual identity—an awareness and acceptance of one's basic biological nature as a man or a woman. Because one's sex is a biological fact about which one can do little, sexual identity conflicts are likely to create significant problems in the development of a confident, secure overall identity.

Boys and girls come out to play ... and find something more interesting than bowling to talk about.

It is important to distinguish between *sexual identity* and *sex-role behaviour*. Appropriate behaviour as a man or a woman need not mean rigid conformity to sex-role stereotypes such as that of the ambitious, self-reliant, assertive, but not very sensitive male, and the affectionate, gentle, sensitive, but not very assertive female. There is no biological reason why men and women should not be capable both of independence and a reasonable kind of assertiveness as well as cherishing and sensitivity. Indeed, the findings of a number of recent scientific investigations suggest that young men and women who are androgynous (that is, who combine within themselves both 'masculine' and 'feminine' characteristics) score higher on measures of self-esteem, do better in their academic work in school and college, have better relations with the opposite sex, and are more self-reliant and independent and less conforming than more purely masculine or feminine types.[8]

Although I agree generally with this view, I think it is also important in our enthusiasm for women's—and men's—liberation to avoid imposing new sets of stereotypes—even some 'ideal' androgynous balance—on all boys and girls, men and women. The ultimate aim of any process of socialisation should be to permit each adolescent to develop his or her unique potential as a human being, consistent with the rights of others.

A changing world

Mastering the developmental tasks of adolescence has become more complex and difficult to accomplish in today's world. Both parents and adolescents face a rapidly changing, often deeply divided society, in which adult authority has been weakened, the validity of many traditional social institutions is being questioned and few consistent social blueprints remain to guide them. Sexual and social roles of men and women may change, as indeed they are changing today; the responsibilities and privileges associated with independence may change; the difficulties of projecting the vocational needs of the future may increase; and the kinds of personal and social identity fitting to both today's and tomorrow's world may alter. Nevertheless, the tasks themselves remain fundamentally the same.

The ease with which a young person is able to master these tasks depends on many factors, past and present. These include the kind and nature of peer-group influences, whether socially normative or deviant; the degree of support and understanding provided by social institutions, such as the school; the interest of non-familial adults, including teachers, employers, counsellors, and friends; and the general climate of society as a whole, including its attitude towards young people.

But parents are, as they have always been in the West, the single most important external influence in aiding or hindering the average adolescent in arriving at a satisfactory identity. Being a parent—or an adolescent—has never been easy, and in today's world of rapid change it is even more of a challenge than it used to be. If this book can help parents and other adults towards a better understanding of today's adolescents—or adolescents to a better understanding of themselves and their peers—it will have served its purpose.

A man's body, not a child's any more— and with it in tribal societies comes the award of a stable, consistent role.

2 Growing up: the body

Despite the variations in the way the young are treated in different societies, one aspect of adolescence is universal: the physical and physiological changes of puberty that mark its beginning, and the young person's need to find some way to adjust to and master these changes. No other developmental event is more dramatic nor more challenging. Indeed, in the few short years of early adolescence, one has to cope with a virtual biological revolution within oneself: rapid growth in height and weight, changing bodily dimensions, hormonal changes leading to increased sex drive, the development of primary and secondary sexual characteristics, further growth of mental ability. Parents, teachers, peers—and society generally—may help or hinder one's adjustment to these changes, and may influence whether they become a source of pride or of anxiety and confusion. But they cannot alter the fact that those changes will occur and that, in one way or another, the adolescent must learn to cope with them.

The development of a sense of one's identity as a person calls for, among other things, a feeling of the consistency and stability of the self—not only at a particular moment, but also over time. One needs to feel that the person one is today is similar to or at best a development of the person one was yesterday.

This feeling of self-consistency is threatened by the many rapid internal changes of puberty. Unlike the younger child, whose physical growth is gradual and orderly, the adolescent is likely, over quite a short time, to find that he feels a stranger to the self with which he or she has been familiar since early childhood. The process of integrating these dramatic physical changes successfully into an emerging sense of a stable, self-confident personal identity may be a prolonged and difficult one. There is no doubt that it could often be made considerably easier, less set about with unnecessary worries, if young people (and their parents) had a clearer idea of the true nature of the physical and physiological changes of their puberty and later adolescence. But in all too many cases, adolescents suffer needlessly because of persistent but patently false myths about this crucial transition from childhood to full membership in an adult world.

Hormones and the biological clock

The term 'puberty' derives from the Latin word *pubertas*, meaning 'age of manhood'. It refers to the first phase of adolescence, when sexual maturation becomes evident. The onset of puberty becomes most readily apparent with the initial appearance of pubic hair and, in girls, the first signs of elevation of the breasts (the 'bud' stage). In fact, by this stage the process has already been going on for some time internally, with an increase in the size of the testes in boys and an enlargement of the ovaries in girls.

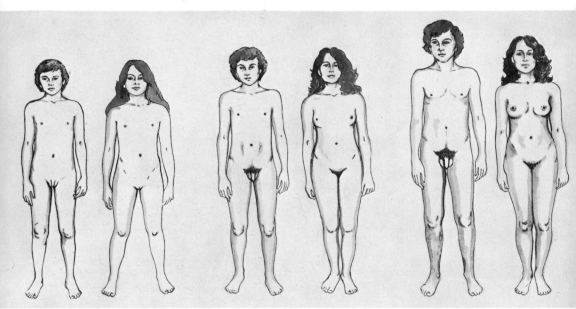

Average appearance of boys and girls at ages 10 (left), 14 and 18 (right). Individuals may differ markedly from these models— for example a boy of 14 may still look like 10 or already seem to be 18.

The intricate sequence of events producing physical growth and sexual maturation is controlled by hormones secreted by the endocrine glands, and these themselves are triggered by signals originating in the hypothalamus, an important co-ordinating centre in the brain. This can only occur when the hypothalamus is sufficiently mature. The signal stimulates the pituitary gland, located immediately below the base of the brain, to release hormones which themselves have stimulating effects on other endocrine glands in the body. It is from these that more hormones finally come which are to affect physical growth and sexual development.

Among them are thyroxine from the thyroid gland, cortisol from the adrenal gland, and sex hormones, including androgens (the masculinising hormones, including testosterone), oestrogens (the feminising hormones), and progestins or gestagens (the pregnancy hormones). By means of complex feedback mechanisms, these and other hormones stimulate and accelerate the many physical and physiological developments of puberty and adolescence.[1]

The growth spurt

The term 'adolescent growth spurt' refers to the accelerated rate of increase in height and weight that accompanies puberty. The age at which the growth spurt (and puberty generally) begins varies widely even among perfectly normal children. In boys, the growth spurt may begin as early as $10\frac{1}{2}$ or as late as 16: some boys may have almost completed their physical development before it begins in others, without any implication that either one or the other is abnormal. For the average boy, however, rapid acceleration in growth begins at about $12\frac{1}{2}$, reaches its fastest rate at 14, and then declines to pre-growth rates around the age of 14. The growth spurt begins on average two years earlier in girls.

The shape of things to come

Changes in height and weight are accompanied by changes in body proportions in both boys and girls. The head, hands, and feet reach adult size first. In turn, the arms and legs grow faster than trunk length, which is completed last. As the English paediatrician, Dr. James Tanner, says, 'A boy stops growing out of his trousers (at least in length) a year before he stops growing out of his jackets'.[2]

These differences in the rate of growth of different parts of the body largely account for the temporary feelings of awkwardness felt by some adolescents, especially those who are growing fastest. For brief periods, some young people may feel that their hands and feet are too big, or that they are 'all legs'. Thoughtless comments by adults will not help.

Sex differences

Sex differences in body shape also are magnified during early adolescence. Although girls have wider hips than boys even in childhood, the difference becomes pronounced with the onset of puberty. Conversely, boys develop thicker as well as larger bones, more muscle tissue, and broader shoulders. Partly because of this, boys become and remain much stronger than girls as adolescence proceeds. There are, however, other reasons for the boy's relatively greater strength: relative to their size, boys develop larger hearts and lungs, a higher systolic blood pressure, a greater capacity for carrying oxygen in the blood, and a lower heart rate while resting. They are also chemically more resistant to fatigue.

Nutritional needs

Many discouraged parents, with a wary eye on the ever-rising cost of food, have the feeling that rapidly growing adolescents, particularly boys, are 'eating us out of house and home'. As can be seen in the accompanying table, on the average boys need more calories at every age than girls. However, a large, very active girl will obviously have greater nutritional needs than a small, inactive boy. (The problems of adolescents who overeat or who eat too little will be discussed in Chapter Nine.)

TABLE

Recommended daily dietary allowances (calories)

	Age	Weight (pounds)	Height (inches)	Calories
Boys	11–14	97	63	2800
	15–18	134	69	3000
	19–22	147	69	3000
Girls	11–14	97	62	2100
	15–18	119	65	2100
	19–22	128	65	2000

Sexual maturation

Although there may be some individual—and perfectly normal—variations in the sequence of events leading to sexual maturity, the following are the typical orders of progression.

In boys, the testes and scrotum begin to increase in size. Pubic hair begins to appear. The penis begins to enlarge (about the same time as the growth spurt starts). Voice deepens as the larynx grows. Hair begins to appear under the arms and on the upper lip. Sperm production increases, and nocturnal emission

Until the voice satisfactorily 'breaks', such enterprises are full of hazards.

(ejaculation of semen during sleep) may occur. Pubic hair becomes pigmented. Prostate gland enlarges.

A number of normal characteristics of sexual maturation may be a source of embarrassment or anxiety to the male adolescent. During the process of voice change (which can be abrupt or gradual), the larynx (Adam's apple) grows larger and the vocal chords virtually double in length. As a result, the boy's voice drops about an octave in tone. It takes at least two years for the average boy to gain full control of this change, during which there may be sudden jumps from a deep bass to a high-pitched squeak. It is easy, but unhelpful, for adults to make fun of this.

In all adolescent boys, there are increases in the size of the areola (the area surrounding the nipple): in some (perhaps 20 to 30 per cent), there is also a distinct enlargement of the breast itself about midway through adolescence, which usually disappears in about a year. This enlargement may cause some boys anxiety about their masculinity, and reassurance about its normality and transitoriness is desirable. They are not going to turn into girls. Likewise some prepubescent boys may show a tendency to rounded hips, which may reinforce the anxiety; but in all normal circumstances this, too, disappears after the onset of the growth spurt. To know this is, in most cases, to forestall a potential misery: a little knowledge is a comforting thing.

In girls, as with boys, there may be normal variations in the sequential order of sexual maturation, but the typical pattern is as follows. Rudimentary elevation of the breast (the so-called bud stage of development) and rounding of the hips. Initial appearance of downy (non-pigmented) pubic hair. Increase in size of the uterus and vagina, the labia and clitoris. Pigmented pubic hair well-developed; moderate amount of axillary (body)

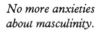

No more anxieties about masculinity.

hair. Further development of breasts; nipple pigmentation; increases in size of areola. Menarche, or onset of menstruation (almost always after the peak rate of growth in height has occurred, and related quite closely to body weight). Further maturation of breasts and growth of axillary hair. Period of 'adolescent sterility' ends, and girl becomes capable of conception (usually about a year or so after menarche).

The vagaries of young appetites can produce extreme variations in body shapes . . .

Like their male counterparts, adolescent girls frequently harbour a number of anxieties about their bodies during this period of rapid physical change. They may worry—but usually less these days than formerly—whether their breasts will be 'too big' or 'too small'. Breast size has in fact nothing to do with the capacity either for breast-feeding or sexual arousal. Nevertheless, some girls with larger breasts may attempt to hide them with loose-fitting clothing or by standing stoop-shouldered, while others may urge boys on by self-conscious displays in tight sweaters, often as a way of reassuring themselves of their desirability. Similarly, some girls with small breasts may wonder why they are 'different', whether they will appeal to boys, or whether they will be capable of having children or of being sexually aroused.

A few girls worried about aspects of their maturation may develop a 'reactive sexuality'. This is a pursuit of sexual experience not so much for its own sake as to reassure themselves of their sexual normality. Adolescent girls may also be concerned about such things as the size of their hips; and many, as we shall see in the next section, may be anxious about the physical, psychological and social aspects of menstruation. Accurate and freely given knowledge of normal development and its many possible variations can help to dispel much unnecessary distress.

Menstruation

Increasing numbers of contemporary girls seem able to accept the onset of menstruation calmly. Some look forward to it. In the words of one older adolescent girl, 'I began to think of it as a symbol. When I got my period, I would be a *woman*.' But many other girls look on this normal—and inevitable—development negatively as 'something women just have to put up with'.[3]

One common reason for these negative attitudes is the image of the experience held by others. If a girl's parents and friends act as though she requires sympathy for her 'plight'—and the most common of the euphemisms for menstruation is 'the curse'—the girl herself is likely to react in a similar fashion. Another reason is lack of adequate preparation for menarche (the onset of menstruation). If her mother waits until menstruation has actually started before explaining its function, a girl may be surprised and shocked by the sudden appearance of menstrual blood, and think that she has injured herself. Some girls have even thought they were dying. Such distress is fortunately much rarer in today's social climate, with its more open acceptance of human sexuality. But it still happens.

. . . but uniform training can get them down to uniform shapes.

Negative reactions to menstruation may also stem from physical discomfort during the early years of puberty. A number of girls experience headache, backache, cramp, feelings of fullness, perhaps generalised abdominal pain. In most cases such initial disturbances either disappear or are greatly reduced as puberty progresses and menstruation becomes more regular. If they do not do so in the normal course of events, medical assistance will usually improve matters.

It is important not to exaggerate the significance of such physical or psychological effects. Girls brought up expecting to feel weak, sick or depressed before and during their periods, and to be unable to engage in normal activities (including vigorous physical exercise), will, not surprisingly, respond as they are expected to. This can lead to using menstruation as an excuse for retreating from normal activities, for gaining attention, or for avoiding other problems. A healthy girl can exercise, go to classes, parties, or do anything she likes while she menstruates.

There are, of course, other reasons why an adolescent girl may react negatively to menstruation. If she resents or fears growing up, or if she has been unable to establish a satisfactory feminine identification, she may be disturbed by the unmistakable message that menstruation provides—that she is a developing woman and there is nothing she can do to change that fact.

'*Practising to be a beautiful lady*'.

Much of this could be avoided or minimised if parents employed a wise and understanding approach and showed pride and pleasure in their daughter's greater maturity. The mother usually plays the major part in this, but fathers can be very helpful too—like the one described by Wardell Pomeroy: '[he] observed the occasion of his daughter's first menstruation by

*Preaching
complementariness.*

bringing her flowers and making a little ceremony of the fact that she had now become a young lady. That daughter could not help feeling proud and good about becoming an adolescent.'[4]

Erection, ejaculation and nocturnal emission

A boy's capacity for erection of the penis and for pleasurable genital stimulation is present from infancy, but only with the onset of puberty and the associated increases in testosterone (male hormone) levels do sexual urges become strong and insistent. Erections become far more frequent, and are likely to be aroused by a wide variety of stimuli, some of which are patently sexual but others much less obviously so. The younger male in fact 'inhabits a libidinized life-space where almost anything can take on a sexual meaning'.[5] Boys may be proud of their capacity for erection as a symbol of emerging virility; but its uncontrollability may also be a potent cause of social or—certainly into the quite recent past—even religious anxiety. They may become apprehensive about dancing with a girl, or having to stand up in class, or even travel in a bus or train. They may be unaware that other boys, too, show this apparent lack of control. Some may even believe that erection is in itself evidence of sin.

All this is likely to be compounded by the body's production—and emission—of seminal fluid: the adolescent boy's first ejaculation is likely to occur within a year of the onset of the growth spurt (around age 14, although it may occur as early as 11 or as late as 16), and may take place as a result of masturbation or nocturnal emission (ejaculation of seminal fluid during sleep, the so-called 'wet dream') or of spontaneous waking orgasm. A boy who has previously masturbated, with accompanying pleasant sensations but without ejaculation, may indeed be taken by surprise by his initial ejaculation of seminal fluid and wonder whether it is harmful. It is important that such fears should be forestalled by adequate information. It is not enough to assume that boys will be already knowledgeable by the onset of puberty. Ignorance is a long time dying.

The 'wet dream', an experience common to almost all males, may produce anxieties in adolescent boys, to the point where they may be afraid to sleep on strange beds or even their own if they think their parents disapprove of sexuality. Nocturnal emission occurs more frequently among youths without other sexual outlets, such as masturbation, petting to orgasm, or intercourse, and may or may not be accompanied by overtly erotic dreams, which may cause puzzlement or guilt.

A significant number of boys, particularly those who are late maturers, or those whose penises are (or are *thought* to be) smaller than average, may worry about their supposed deficiency. Early maturers, or those with larger penises, may easily intensify such worries by boasting of their own endowment. But the truth is that penis size has nothing whatsoever to do with sexual potency or the capacity to provide sexual satisfaction. Nevertheless this preoccupation with physical conformation may assume considerable importance to the adolescent.

25

Being different

As the adolescent moves away from dependence primarily on the family and towards the peer group as a major source of security and social status, conformity to peer group standards becomes more important, not only in social behaviour but in appearance and physical skills. Deviation from the idealised peer group

Time out from the struggle.

norms in body build, facial features, physical abilities—even, at times, in such seemingly irrelevant matters as whether one's hair is straight or curly—may be a source of great distress to an adolescent.

Adults may wonder how an adolescent boy can spend hours before the mirror attempting to find just the right way to comb his hair, or why an adolescent girl worries about a perceived skin blemish that the adult cannot even see. These preoccupations may seem, and indeed be, silly; for the adolescent, however, they may be matters of overwhelming significance. It is important for parents and other adults dealing with adolescents to realise that the young person's self-image is not always based on objective reality. A young girl who is really rather beautiful may see herself as unattractive because she has been told for years that she 'looks just like' a relative she resents. A boy who is physically of average size and strength may feel himself to be smaller or weaker than he is because he feels inadequate generally and has low self-esteem. The opposite may also be the case. A boy or girl who has high self-esteem generally—who has been loved and respected or highly individualised, as a child—may be little bothered by not fitting the stereotyped image of contemporary feminine beauty or masculine achievement; but such indifference, though admirable, may not help its owner to cope successfully with the disapproval too frequently handed out to 'loners' in a conforming society.

Early and late maturers

Young people vary widely in the age at which they reach puberty: at 14, one may be physically well on the way to adulthood while another may still look—and sometimes feel—like a child. Such discordances are perfectly normal, and do not affect the eventual achievement of full physical and sexual maturity; but they can easily affect the view adolescents take of themselves and the way they are viewed by others.

In general, early or late maturing appears to have a greater effect on boys than on girls. Adults and other adolescents tend to think of the 14- or 15-year-old boy who looks 17 or 18 as older than he actually is and are likely, therefore, to expect more mature behaviour from him than they would from a physically less developed boy of the same age. Because there is less of a physical discrepancy between an early maturing boy and most girls his own age (because of the earlier growth spurt in girls), he may become involved sooner and with more self-confidence in boy–girl relationships. Furthermore, a physically more developed boy has an advantage in many activities, especially athletics. So although a boy who matures faster than most of his peers may feel somehow different from them, he is not likely to feel insecure about the difference. He may even come to esteem himself as 'superior' to his less-developed peers.

By contrast, a late-maturing boy is more likely to be 'treated as a child', a fact which may infuriate him, even while he continues to behave immaturely. He is likely to have a harder time in achieving recognition in athletics and other physical activities, as well as in his relations with girls. Perhaps most painful of all, he may wonder when, if ever, he will reach full physical and sexual maturity and be entitled to the respect, from peers and elders, that he believes his identity deserves.

Not surprisingly, this can often result in personality differences between early and late maturers. Long-term research studies have found that boys who mature late tend to be less poised, more tense and talkative, and more self-conscious and affected in their manner than early maturers.[6,7] They are also likely to be more restless, more 'over-eager', more impulsive, more bossy and more 'attention-seeking'.

Early maturers, on the other hand, appear more reserved, self-assured, matter-of-fact, and likely to engage easily in socially appropriate behaviour. They are also more likely to be able to laugh at themselves.

In psychological tests, late maturers were found to have more feelings of inadequacy, poorer self-concepts, and more feelings of being rejected or dominated by others. Somewhat paradoxically, they are more likely to combine persisting dependency needs with a seemingly rebellious search for independence and freedom from parental and social restraints. In other words, late maturers appear more likely to prolong the typical adolescent independence-dependence conflict than early maturers. Such differences have been shown to persist into adulthood.

Much can be done by parents, teachers and others to minimise the anxiety and other negative psychological effects of late maturing. They can make a conscious effort to avoid the trap of treating a late maturer as younger than he really is. They can help him to realise that his slower maturation is perfectly normal—that he will indeed 'grow up' and be just as physically and sexually masculine as his peers. And they can help him to achieve success in activities where physical size and strength are not a handicap.

Among girls, the effects of early or late maturing are generally less, and more variable.[8] Although early-maturing girls tend to be somewhat more relaxed, more self-confident, less anxious, more secure—in a word, better 'adjusted'—the differences are not large. Why the differences should be greater among boys than among girls is something of a mystery. One reason, however, may be that our society's expectations for adolescent boys are clearer and less ambiguous than for girls.

Past puppy-love,
on the way to passion.

In boys, early maturing means greater strength and physical prowess—and, eventually, active sexual behaviour. In girls, our

expectations in Western societies are less clearly defined. Is early sexual maturity a help or a hindrance? Is sexual activity at an earlier age than peers good or bad? Is the girl's adjustment aided by having to deal with the complex feelings aroused by the onset of menstruation and the adaptations it requires when most of her peers are still more like 'little girls'?

Our society often gives girls mixed messages on these matters. The girl who is sexually attractive at an early age will be more likely to attract the attention of older boys. But is this desirable? There is always the danger that she may be lured by the immediate rewards of dating older boys into failure to continue developing mature relationships with other girls her own age, or developing as an individual in her own right. She may also come to feel that she is gaining attention merely as 'a sex object' rather than as a complete person. Perhaps worse, she may come to believe that being pretty, sexy and having superficial social skills is all that is needed to be truly grown up.

3   Mental growth

The dramatic advances of adolescents in their physical development are accompanied by equally impressive, if less obvious, gains in mental ability. The average 14- or 15-year-old can handle easily and efficiently many kinds of intellectual tasks or problems that the average 10-year-old would find impossible—or at least very difficult—to master, but do not be too hopeful that this will include remembering to tidy a bedroom or put the cap back on the toothpaste.

Intelligence—cleverness, mental ability, brightness: there is no agreement about what it consists of, although we all recognise it when we see it—manifests itself in many different ways. Most people will be found to be relatively better at one kind of mental ability and less good at another, perhaps skilled in verbal ability, but poorer in tasks involving arithmetic or understanding how mechanical objects work. The designers of most intelligence tests therefore try to measure as wide a range of mental abilities as possible, hoping that an aggregate of measurements for each of these abilities will give an estimate of a person's intelligence general enough to be compared with the estimates for other people, or with the estimate made for the same person at a different time of life. There are serious dangers in placing too much reliance on such measurements; but they do seem to have a practical validity which is very useful in, for example, comparing mental growth at different stages of life.

Thus, when large numbers of the same subjects are repeatedly tested over many years, it is found that overall mental ability increases quite rapidly throughout the years of childhood and adolescence and then slows down noticeably in adulthood. Such tests also show that the years between puberty and adulthood are very important to a person's intellectual or cognitive development. It is in this period that much of our capacity to acquire and utilise knowledge—though not the knowledge itself—approaches its peak efficiency. Specific abilities do not develop—or decline— at the same rate which is why failure to develop intellectual potential in the formative years may be hard to remedy later. Those that reflect 'pure' biological capability, including speed of perception, analytic power and intellectual flexibility, develop more rapidly during childhood and adolescence, and decline somewhat earlier and more rapidly during the adult years, than abilities that are more likely to be influenced by experience, such

*On the internal map
of cognitive ability,
new territory is
marked out every day.*

as word fluency. This partly explains why mathematicians tend to reach their peaks much earlier in life than, say, historians or philosophers.

Intelligence and IQ

At this point it is necessary to distinguish between intelligence itself and the 'intelligence quotient' (IQ)—if only because it is obvious that, while a five-year-old and a 50-year-old may both be labelled 'IQ 125', their actual mental abilities must differ greatly. Scores on IQ tests tend to remain relatively stable largely

Grandma knows best—but the child learns better.

because they are designed to match the developmental stage of the person being tested and to measure *relative* brightness in camparison with others at the same stage. It follows that an IQ of 125 at age 5 (i.e. 25 per cent better score than the bulk of the test population) is likely to persist as an IQ of 125 at age 50. IQ is not a measure of *absolute* mental ability and has little to do with wisdom or the general ability to cope with one's environment. It does, however, give a reasonably good indication of potential academic ability.

Genetic influences on mental ability

We become the kinds of people we are as the result of a continuing interaction between our growing, changing bodies and our environment—physical, psychological, and social. Variations in either our biology or environment may influence the outcome. For example, the fact that one person is physically stronger than another may be owed to his having a more athletic constitution, with larger bones and greater muscle mass, or to rigorous exercise and training—or, of course, to both. Having an athletic constitution, in turn, may be largely a matter of heredity—the particular genes one is born with—although other factors such as good nutrition and the absence of debilitating diseases can be crucially involved.

Intellectual ability appears to work in much the same way. We know that the development of a child's mental abilities can be aided by good learning experiences and hindered by the lack of a stimulating environment, by parental indifference to the child's progress, or by poor nutrition and illness. But there is also

Lack of a more stimulating environment may mean that this child never achieves his possible abilities.

evidence that a child's or adolescent's ultimate intellectual potential is influenced by heredity—by genetic factors. The more closely two people are related genetically, the closer their IQ scores are likely to be.

In brief, an individual is likely to be at least as bright as his or her IQ score would indicate; but—because of limitations on test performance ranging from anxiety or lack of interest to cultural deprivation—we cannot be half so certain he or she is not *more* intelligent.

Sex difference in intelligence

Although adolescent boys and girls show no consistent difference in *overall* intelligence, there are some differences in specific competences. From about 10 or 11 years of age, girls tend to outscore boys on tests of *verbal ability*, while boys score higher on *visual–spatial* tasks (for example, visualising how an object in space would look from a different angle; seing how a set of gears works; or solving mazes). From about the age of twelve or thirteen, boys also score somewhat higher in *mathematical ability*. It is not clear how much these differences are due to genetic influences and how much they are the result of sexual stereotyping—that is, the expectations society has of what boys and girls each *should* be good at.[1]

Moving into top gear

Around the age of 12 (but with marked individual variations), young people enter what the Swiss psychologist Piaget labelled 'the stage of formal operations'.[2] During this stage the adolescent gains a number of important capabilities not generally present in the childhood years. Probably the most basic of these involves a shift of emphasis in his or her thinking from the *real* to the *possible*—from what merely *is* to what might be—and the ability simultaneously to consider a variety of possibilities in a thorough and objective fashion as well as to think in abstract terms. This vastly increases the adolescent's capacity to deal with himself and with the surrounding world.

The development of formal operational thought is related not only to age but to overall intelligence, developing somewhat earlier in adolescents with higher IQs. But some adolescents and adults may never develop true formal operational thinking, either because of limited ability or because of cultural limitations. Finally, formal operational thought is not an 'all-or-nothing' affair: a really gifted adolescent girl or boy is likely to display

In adolescence, such play-acting can be the exploration of the possible as well as just fun.

greater imagination, greater flexibility and more precision in the exercise of formal operational thinking than his or her peers, although the basic processes involved in both cases are similar. Like any other tool, it can be used with artistry or clumsiness.

Rebel with a cause

It would be hard to overestimate the importance of the changes in mental ability that take place during adolescence, particularly of the shift in the direction of formal operational thinking. Without these changes, the young person would be unable to deal adequately with many of the intellectual demands made upon him or her during these years.

But many other aspects of the adolescent's development also depend on the cognitive advances during this period. Changes in the nature of parent-child relationships, emerging personality characteristics and psychological defence mechanisms, mounting concerns with social, political and personal values, even the development of a sense of personal identity, are all strongly influenced by the growth of cognitive skill.[3]

One of the most important aspects of the emergence of formal operational thought is the ability to grasp not only the immediate state of things but also the possible state they might or could assume. The implications of this change alone are enormous.

For example, there is the adolescent's newfound and frequently wearing talent for discovering that his or her parents, previously simply 'there', or even idolised as the fount of wisdom and virtue, have feet of clay. Their values are questioned, they are compared with other 'more understanding' or less 'square' parents, and are accused of 'hypocritical' inconsistencies between professed values and behaviour. This criticism depends at least partly on the adolescent's increased cognitive ability. As David Elkind, an expert on this topic, comments, 'The awareness of the discrepancy between the actual and the possible ... helps to make the adolescent a rebel. He is always comparing the possible with the actual and discovering that the actual is ... wanting.'[4]

The relentless criticism by many adolescents of existing social, political and religious systems, and their preoccupation with devising often elaborate or highly theoretical alternative systems, also depends to a considerable extent on their emerging capacity for formal operational thought.

Such deep concerns are often couched in deplorable language and tend to be most characteristic of our brightest young people. This is due as much to their greater cognitive capability as to their more 'permissive' upbringing, 'affluence' or 'politicisation'. Much of an adolescent's apparently passionate concern with the deficiencies of parents and the social order, and with the creation of 'viable alternatives', often turns out to be primarily verbal— more a matter of word than deed. This is probably at least partly because this stage of development is still relatively new and has not yet been fully integrated into the adolescent's total adaptation to life. Many adolescents voice their strong devotion to humanitarian causes, but then do little to advance them.

At the same time, it is important to recognise the positive aspects of the young person's newly acquired ability to conceptualise, to reason abstractly about hypothetical situations and to embrace 'instant' convictions with passion. Not only is the exercise of this ability a pleasure in itself; it also provides valuable and necessary practice in the development of reasoning skills and critical abilities that will be needed throughout life. What may appear to the weary adult as 'a vain rehashing or sterile questioning of old worn-out problems, corresponds in reality—for the youngster—to youthful explorations, and true discoveries'.[5]

Personality

'At last I've grasped what it's all about!'

Adolescent cognitive development is also reflected in the young person's attitudes to himself or herself, and in the personality characteristics likely to become prominent during this period. Many adolescents at this stage become more introspective and analytical. They are likely to be concerned with such philosophic puzzles as whether the world that they perceive actually exists and, indeed, whether they themselves are real or a product of consciousness.

Adolescents often appear egocentric in their thought and behaviour. At this stage they are able to realise that other people

Are they real people to each other, or just the embodiment of each other's dreams?

are capable of thought processes similar to their own. But, at least initially, they are not likely to differentiate clearly between the content of their own thoughts and those of others. Consequently, because young people's concerns at this age are likely to be focused on themselves, they are likely to conclude that other people, including their peers, are equally obsessed with their behaviour and appearance. 'It is this belief that others are preoccupied with his appearance and behaviour that constitutes the egocentrism of the adolescent.'[6]

A number of other common adolescent characteristics appear to be at least partly related to cognitive development. Frequent use of irony, puns and *double entendre* can be understood partly as an exercise of the young person's newfound talent for thinking on a symbolic level.

The adolescent's mental growth also plays an important part in the emergence of a well-defined sense of identity. The ability to consider the possible as well as what currently is, to try out alternative solutions to problems, to look further into the future, all help the young person to address the central questions, 'Who am I?', 'Who do I want to be?', and 'What are my chances of getting there?' The adolescent can try out many different roles, seeking to find those which seem personally most comfortable, rewarding, or challenging, and those which appear realistic or unrealistic in the light of his or her talents, skills, and opportunities. Indeed, just being aware that there is a part of the self that can reason, formulate and modify assumptions, consider alternatives, and arrive at conclusions, however tentative, helps to foster the sense of identity.

Cogito, ergo sum

Even the quality of adolescent love reflects to some degree the cognitive changes of adolescence. Many young people fall in love, not so much with the reality of the other person, as with a carefully constructed fantasy. This fantasy is based on all kinds of untested assumptions, many of which may have little basis in fact. 'The girl of my dreams . . .' extolled in popular songs is often just that.

The expansion of mental ability that takes place in adolescence can make it a time of unparalleled creativity, challenge, and intellectual adventure. It is unfortunate that instead of encouraging these possibilities, we so often pour cold water on them, urging the young person instead to be 'practical', or 'realistic'. By this we often mean giving up dreams and lowering expectations of what it is possible to achieve. Many adolescent dreams may never be fulfilled, but just having had them can make the remainder of a person's life fuller and richer.

4

Adolescents and their parents

Adolescence is likely to be a challenging and sometimes trying time for those undergoing the experience and for their parents. It could hardly be otherwise, in view of the many changes taking place during these years in both child and parent and in their relationship with one another.

In their own way, parents, too, may face an 'identity crisis'. The parent of the average adolescent is entering middle age. At a time when their children are approaching the peak of their physical and sexual vigour, parents are faced with the fact that they have passed their own physical peaks, and that the rest of the road slopes downhill, however gently at first. In a society as obsessed with youth as our own—and as scornful of old age—the prospect can sometimes be a painful one.

Their children's adolescent years can be a time of 'agonising reappraisal' for parents in other ways as well. Husbands are likely to be aware that if they have not realised whatever dreams they may have had of vocational or social glory by their early forties, or shortly thereafter, they are not likely to realise them. Similarly, a wife who may have suppressed other life goals in the interest of childrearing or—still more difficult to cope with—who may have used her relationship with her children as a compensation for other disappointments, must face the fact that her children will soon be gone. What, she may ask, will she do then? Indeed, *who* will she be then?

This is also a time when parents and their adolescent sons and daughters must learn to establish new kinds of relationships with each other. Parents must be able to recognise—and encourage—the adolescent's needs for increased independence. Continuing to think of their adolescent young simply as 'our darling baby' or 'our little boy' and treating them accordingly is a prescription for later disaster, whether it takes the form of explosive rebellion or continued and increasingly inappropriate dependence.

At the same time, however, it is vital to recognise that true independence is not built in a day. Dependent needs continue to exist, often in uneasy and fragile alliance with needs for independence. Partly because so many things are changing in the adolescent's world, he or she urgently needs a base of security

Are they models for their
sons, the living spirits
of 'don't'—*or just*
a pair of dummies?

39

and stability in home and parents—something to take for granted while more urgent concerns are worked out. Along with the increasing independence comes an inevitable shift in the emotional relationships between parent and child. If the young person is eventually going to achieve emotional, social and sexual maturity, he or she must gradually begin shifting to peers—to 'best friends' and boy friends or girl friends—some of the intimate emotional attachment previously reserved largely for parents.

The shift in emotional relationships from parents to 'best friends' can be puzzling and awkward.

Obviously adaptation to this new kind of relationship is going to be more difficult for some parents—and adolescents—than for others. Mothers and fathers who feel unloved by their spouses or their friends may be reluctant to see their children begin leading their own lives and forming new emotional attachments outside the family, especially if the child is providing compensation for other frustrations in life. Some parents consciously desire that their children lead happy and rewarding lives, but keep them tied to their apron strings through jealousy. Unconsciously, they do not want their children to enjoy good times that they themselves are missing.

Even under the most favourable circumstances the adjustment to the young person's emotional separation from the family is bound to have its painful moments for both parents and children. Inevitably, and quite properly, there will be occasional feelings of loss and longings for a simpler time when there was 'just the family'.

Adolescent 'storm and stress': myth or reality?
The popular view of adolescence among some doctors and in many books and films is of a period of great 'storm and stress'.

Yet more broadly representative studies indicate that while this is certainly the case with some young people, including some of the most sensitive and gifted of them as well as some of the most maladjusted, it is not true of the majority of adolescents. Indeed, some investigators have expressed dismay at the number of young people who have undergone 'a premature identity consolidation', characterised by a rather bland acceptance of things as they are and 'a general unwillingness to take psychic risk'.[1]

The generations separate: new alliances are marked by dress-style, hairstyle, life style.

This does not mean that these adolescents are without problems or conflicts, however—only that such 'symptoms' will tend, with few exceptions, to be mild and transitory.

The family at war

Conflicts with parents are natural and to be expected, particularly during the earlier years of adolescence. For one thing, as their mental horizons expand, adolescents begin to see that the family's values and way of life are not the only possible ones.

Younger children usually have the conviction that 'how we do it at our house' is the right, the only possible, way. When a mother or father says, 'The Joneses are pretty odd people,' the younger child will generally accept it as a statement of fact.[2]

Not so the adolescent, who is capable of perceiving not only that there is room for alternative values, beliefs, or ways of doing things, but that the style of other parents may actually be superior to that of their own. It may take a long time, but, ultimately, the young person is likely to conclude that, while parents do not have all the answers, their opinions and knowledge—gained from sometimes bitter experience—can still be helpful and are at least familiar. And sometimes the 'new' people whose style one takes to admiring turn out to be a good deal more odd than one wants or can cope with.

Another common reason for parent-adolescent conflicts during these years is the 'tyranny of habit'. It is often difficult for parents to realise that their little girl or boy is no longer a child, and that rules and regulations that may have been appropriate when their children were younger are no longer so. Even when they do realise it, it is often difficult to break old habits.

One way to prove that 'I'm not a child any more'?

The problem may be further confounded by inconsistencies on the part of the adolescent. As we have noted, adolescents typically have mixed feelings about independence and dependence. At one level, they know that sooner or later they will have to become independent, make their own way in the world, and be responsible for their own actions. In many ways, the prospect of 'freedom' will be appealing.

But the prospect of impending independence and its responsibilities can sometimes be frightening, too; and then the security of continued childhood dependence, the knowledge that a mother or father will somehow 'make things all right', also has its appeal.

These conflicts between independent and dependent needs can lead to sudden and unpredictable swings in attitudes and behaviour. The adolescent may be surprisingly mature, independent and responsible one moment, and childlike and undependable the next. Just when a mother and father think their son or daughter has earned greater freedom, something may happen to make the parents doubt whether he or she has grown up at all. Forgetting a vital appointment, getting plans all made for an outing and then deciding not to go, promising to perform some necessary or even important task and then neglecting to do so, indignantly bucking against parental nagging about homework and then failing to prepare for a school examination—these are common causes of the near-despair that at one time or another visits the parents of every adolescent.

Rites of passage

Another reason for some of the conflicts between adolescents and their parents is the lack of clearcut guidelines in contemporary society—for either parents or their children—about what behaviour is appropriate for adolescents at a particular age. What rules *should* parents try to impose, and at what age, about relations with the opposite sex, drinking, driving the family car, going on trips with peers?

In many 'primitive' societies, the privileges and obligations of each age group are clearly spelled out. There also tends to be a more clearly defined boundary between adolescence and adulthood, marked by a 'rite of passage', or initiation ceremony. Completion of this means that the boy or girl is accepted as an adult, though junior, member of society, with the appropriate freedoms and responsibilities granted and expected by the society, not just the parents.

Was life easier for adolescents when the duties and privileges of their age group were well-defined?

No such institutionalised pattern of recognition of the adolescent's impending or achieved maturity is provided in developed industrial societies today. All we have is a hotch-potch

of often inconsistent and loosely-enforced rules, which may vary from community to community across an otherwise unitary society, about when a young person may drink, drive a car, leave school, marry, or own property. 'Society no longer bestows adult status at any one point. Confirmation, Bar Mitzvah, and the coming-out party have lost their significance as puberty rites . . .'[3]

The problem in contemporary society of what to expect of adolescents and how to persuade them to meet the appropriate expectations has been complicated by the rapidity of social, moral and political change in recent years. So swift has this change been in the past several decades that today's adolescents have grown up in a markedly different world from their parents', whose own experiences as children and adolescents may consequently be virtually useless as guidance in understanding their children's needs, problems and goals.

The problem of childrearing has also been made more difficult by rapidly increasing urbanisation and geographic mobility in many industrialised nations. This is particularly true in the

City or suburb,
the urban young will
find a forum
and meeting-place
for their own kind.

United States, where approximately half of all families move every five years, often into unfamiliar communities, far from relatives and friends. America is steadily becoming, in Vance Packard's words, 'a nation of strangers'. In an earlier day, a puzzled parent could more readily turn for help to family members or close friends or others of similar cultural background.

It is not simply a matter of parents gaining a greater feeling of security and direction from living in a close-knit, relatively homogeneous community. Their children are also more likely to accept parental rules, standards and beliefs when they see that these are shared by other significant adults.

But many parents today find it difficult or impossible to communicate closely with other parents; and where these other parents follow different rules, the opportunities for such familiar adolescent 'blackmail' techniques as 'all the other kids are allowed to do it', or 'Susie's parents don't act that way', are significantly increased. Adolescents themselves may also be genuinely confused or sceptical about the diversity they observe in the values, beliefs and practices among peers and parents.

The 'generation gap'

Despite the increased difficulty of rearing children and adolescents in today's world, most parents and young people manage to succeed, not without some ups and downs and worrying times, but without unresolvable conflicts and serious alienation.

There is, as one might reasonably expect for persons at different stages of the life cycle, a 'generation gap'. But it is neither as wide nor as novel as we have been led to believe. Even at the height of the 'youth culture' of the late 1960s, the great majority of both parents and adolescents in the United States expressed the view that, while a generation gap existed, it had clearly been exaggerated.[4]

Backyard togetherness, and a bridging of the generation gap.

Current studies give much the same picture. In a recent survey of American adolescents aged 13–19, most of the sample (87 per

cent of boys and 89 per cent of girls) stated that they had a lot of respect for their parents as people; and nearly as many stated that they had a lot of respect for their parents' ideas and opinions. The percentage acknowledging 'a lot of respect' was somewhat higher for girls than for boys, and higher for younger girls than for older ones.

Only a relatively small minority stated that they did not feel any strong affection for their parents. And only 6 per cent felt that 'My parents don't really like me'. Fewer than a fifth of all adolescents agreed that 'I've pretty much given up on ever being able to get along with my parents'. Indeed, two-thirds of young Americans aged 16–25 consider family 'a very important value', and a similar proportion would 'welcome more emphasis on traditional family ties'.[5]

In most cases, conflicts with parents involve issues of personal freedom. How many parents are familiar with such adolescent complaints as 'I don't see why I have to be home by twelve. None of my friends have to'; 'Why do you let him (her) do it, but not me?'; 'Why do you always treat me like a baby?'; and 'You can't make me!'

And how many adolescents have had their requests greeted with 'We'll see . . .'; 'Why do you want to go around with those boys (girls)?'; 'When you're older, you'll understand . . .'; or 'Because I know what's best.'?

The fact is that, while they may seem earthshaking at the time, most parent-adolescent conflicts are about relatively minor matters. These include getting to bed by a certain time, being able to go to parties or on trips with peers, using the family car, doing chores, spending allowance money, choosing clothes or hair styles, seeing 'too much' of some particular member of the opposite sex and the like.

Trying herself on for size . . .

Parents: very important people

Why do some parents succeed, while others fail? Why do some adolescents grow into adulthood confident, competent, caring, secure in their own sense of identity and in their relations with their families, while others emerge from adolescence direction-less, lacking in independence, low in self-esteem, ineffective, angry and alienated, or victims of psychological disturbance? Obviously there is no simple answer. Many factors may play a part: social disorder, disruptive peer influences, discrimination, poverty, poor schooling, even the genes one was born with.

Nevertheless, an impressive body of research and clinical investigation makes it clear that the single most important influence in helping or hindering the average adolescent to cope with the developmental demands of adolescence in today's world is his or her parents. But what kind of parents? Parents may be loving or rejecting, calm or anxious, rigid or inflexible, involved or uninvolved: but there are two 'dimensions' of parental behaviour that are of particular importance.

Love versus hostility

The first of these dimensions may be labelled *love-hostility*, or *acceptance-rejection*. The need of children and adolescents for loving, caring parents whom they can trust and in whom they can have confidence has been demonstrated repeatedly, both in clinical work and in systematic research with normal, neurotic and delinquent children and adolescents.[6] Without strong and

'It is a wise child that knows its own father ...'

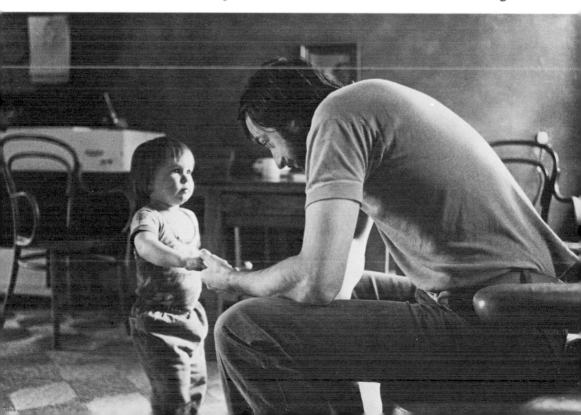

clear manifestations of parental love, the child or adolescent has little chance of developing self-esteem, constructive and rewarding relationships with others, and a confident sense of his or her own identity.

'I have tried to talk to my father, but it seems like he doesn't want to listen. I don't know why. I guess he thinks my problems aren't very important. Anyway, he's pretty busy . . .' (*15-year-old boy.*)

'I can't pick out a future . . . I ran away because our step-dad beat us all the time. . . I can't see any adult I dream to be like . . . I've never seen the good life . . . I am lonely all the time.' (*14-year-old girl, runaway.*)[7]

With real parental warmth and caring, however, the young person is often able to overcome many seemingly insuperable obstacles. As one 14-year-old girl from a poor urban neighbourhood said about her mother, 'She takes a lot of time for her kids and she listens to what you have to say and she's understanding. Some marriages have divorce problems or something, but our parents got along good for 20 years. She seems to always understand . . .'[8]

In many urban settings adolescents, left alone by working parents, are the chief population: what do they think of their lives?

Or this from a 17-year-old, speaking of her family: 'I guess really they're the most important. Because they're always there and I always can go to them and they always say something that will make me feel better. And they support me in my activities and, I don't know, they're just good all around.'[9]

Parental hostility, rejection, or neglect consistently occur more often than acceptance, love, and trust in the backgrounds of children with a very wide variety of problems. These range from intellectual and academic difficulties and impaired social relationships with peers and adults to neurotic disorders, psychosomatic disturbances, and character problems such as delinquency.

'I never could talk to my old man. He just comes home from work and sits there drinking beer and watching television. Besides, he says I'm stupid, and I'll never amount to anything anyway. When I got caught joyriding, he said that was fine with him, they could lock me up and throw away the key . . .' (*16-year-old boy, delinquent.*)

Control versus freedom

Perhaps less obvious, but equally important, is the parents' position on the question of control versus freedom.

To cope effectively with today's and tomorrow's world, adolescents need discipline (ultimately self-discipline). But they also need independence, self-reliance, adaptability, and a strong sense of their own values. Research has shown that these qualities are fostered best by parents who show respect for their children, involve them in family affairs and decision-making, and encourage the development of age-appropriate independence—but who also retain ultimate responsibility with confidence.

Such parents are, in the words of psychologist Diana Baumrind, *authoritative* without being *authoritarian*.[10] They value both autonomous self-will *and* disciplined behaviour. They encourage verbal give-and-take, and when they exercise parental authority in the form of demands or prohibitions, they explain their reasons for doing so. This description by a 16-year-old girl is typical of such parents: 'I guess the thing I think is great about my parents, compared to those of a lot of kids, is that they really listen. And they realise that eventually I'm going to have to live my own life—what I'm going to do with it. A lot of the time when I explain what I want to do, they'll go along with it. Sometimes, they'll warn me of the consequences I'll have to face if I'm wrong, or just give me advice. And sometimes, they just plain tell me no. But when they do, they explain why, and that makes it easier to take . . .'[11]

'Because I said so!': authoritarian parents

In contrast to the authoritative parent is the *authoritarian* (or, in more extreme form, *autocratic*) parent, who just tells the child or adolescent what to do and feels no obligation to explain why. Such parents favour obedience as an absolute virtue, and tend to deal with any attempts at protest with punitive, forceful measures. Any sort of free discussion or two-way interaction between the parent and child is discouraged, in the conviction that the young person should unquestioningly accept the parent's word for what is right.

Some parents may take this stance out of a feeling of hostility, or simply because they can't be bothered. Others, however, may be doing so because they think that this is the way to develop

Adults through the ages never seem to remember the lessons of 1789 and 1917: autocratic rule breeds rebellion.

'respect for authority'. A mistake they make is that, while they may suppress dissent, they do not usually eliminate it. They may even encourage resentment. Many children of autocratic or authoritarian parents—because they aren't given a chance to test out their own ideas or take independent responsibility, and because their opinions aren't treated as worthy of consideration—emerge from adolescence lacking in self-confidence and self-esteem, or unable to be self-reliant, act independently, or think for themselves. As adolescents, the children of authoritarian and autocratic parents are far more likely than the children of authoritative parents to say they felt unwanted by both fathers and mothers. They are also less likely as adolescents and young adults to have a mature conscience, based on internalised, independent moral standards rather than a weakly developed and changeable conscience based more on external rewards and punishments.

Laissez-faire and egalitarian parents

Parents who are *laissez-faire* or who assume a false and exaggerated 'egalitarianism' also fail to provide the kind of support that their adolescent young need in today's world. In several recent studies of middle-class adolescents, high-risk drug use and other forms of socially deviant behaviour were found to occur most frequently among the children of parents who outwardly expressed such values as individuality, self-understanding, and the need for egalitarianism within the family but actually used these proclaimed values to avoid assuming parental responsibility.

By setting up the family as a pseudo-democracy these parents are able to abdicate from decision-making powers, responsibility, and unequal status. But by placing themselves on the footing of peers, they end up leaving their children to drift essentially rudderless in an uncharted sea.

No matter how much children and adolescents may protest at times, they do not really want their parents to be equals. They want and *need* them to be *parents*—friendly, understanding parents, but parents nonetheless, models of *adult* behaviour.

Parents in contemporary society therefore face the problem of steering a delicate course between authoritarianism on the one hand and over-permissiveness, 'egalitarianism', or neglect on the other. But for those who are able to achieve this balance, the results can be rewarding to both parent and child. As an 18-year-old Chicago girl said of her mother, 'She's given me confidence in myself and sometimes she tries to make me understand her point of view. Then when she says something and it's right even though it hurts me, I kind of listen to her even though I pretend I'm not listening, I turn my face; and she makes me believe in myself, even when I'm down.'

Or this from a 16-year-old boy: 'My dad's kind of special I guess. Like he takes me camping, and he sits down and talks to me about trouble at school. He wants to know what I'm doing, where I'm going. He helps me to learn things, and I admire him for being smart and strong and able to handle problems.'

All of this does make sense in today's world. Autocratic patterns of parental behaviour may have been more workable in simpler and less rapidly changing times, when an adolescent could expect to be successful by simply following in a father's or mother's footsteps. Today, however, parents can, under favourable circumstances, still provide their children with models of successful, independent, flexible, realistic behaviour. But they cannot provide detailed blueprints for mastering the changing of a world in headlong transition.

5 Adolescents and sex

Of all the developmental events of adolescence, the most dramatic is the increase in sexual drive and the new and often mysterious feelings and thoughts that accompany it. A major hurdle for both boys and girls at this stage is the successful integration of sexuality with other aspects of the emerging sense of self without having to undergo too much conflict and anxiety. In contemporary society, with its changing sex roles and its peculiar mixture of permissiveness and prudery, this is not an easy task to master.

In early adolescence, at least, the problem is likely to be greater for boys than girls. For reasons that we do not entirely understand—although physiological (including hormonal) and psychological factors are probably both involved—boys are more conscious of specifically sexual impulses than girls, and find them harder to deny.

Sexual drive among girls is likely to be more diffuse and ambiguous, and more intertwined with other needs, such as love, self-esteem, reassurance, and affection. For many younger adolescent girls, a limited temporary denial of sexual impulses may not only be more possible than in the case of boys, 'but may indeed seem to be a more comfortable adaptation'. There are, of course, exceptions. A minority of younger adolescent girls are as preoccupied with sex as boys, and as motivated to find sexual release. For some, this may be a natural response, facilitated by a 'liberated' upbringing. In other cases what appears to be a vigorous pursuit of sexual activity is actually a search for love, recognition or approval, or an expression of rebellion or resentment.

But in spite of these relative differences, boys and girls have much in common in their concerns about sexuality. They want to know about such practical matters as masturbation, sexual intercourse, conception, pregnancy and birth control. Even more important, they want to know how to fit sex into their overall values, and how to have mutually rewarding, constructive relations with others, both of the same and the opposite sex. On these matters, most young people receive little help from the inconsistent, conflict-ridden, sometimes hypocritical world in which they live.

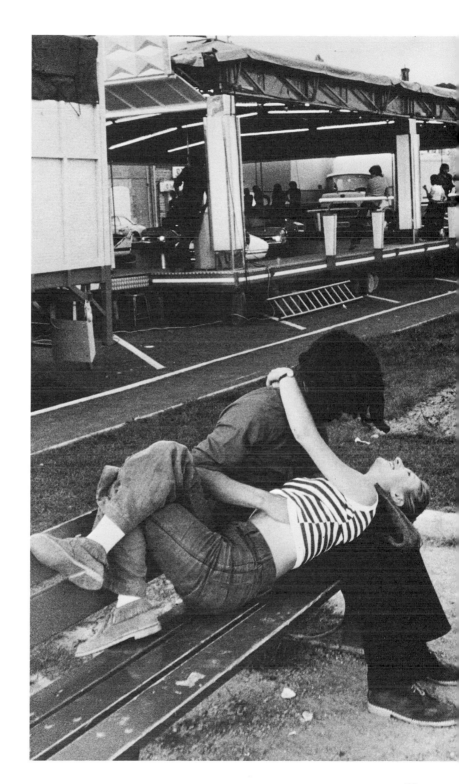

The 'new and mysterious feelings' of the awakened sex drive of adolescence ...

Sex education

A good many adults in Western societies remain adamantly opposed to adequate programmes—sometimes to *any* programmes—of sex education. Some parents believe that sex education, even at high-school level, is dangerously premature for 'impressionable' adolescents and likely to lead them into indiscriminate promiscuity. Others maintain that information

Even 'doing what comes nat'rally' needs a foundation of authoritative information.

about sex should be taught only by parents in the privacy of their own homes. Still others have apparently reached the conclusion that today's adolescents have nothing left to learn about sex—certainly nothing that their parents could teach them. None of these views will stand up to scrutiny.

In the light of the current statistics on premarital intercourse and pregnancy, it is difficult to see how sex education for adolescents could be viewed as in any way 'premature'; and whether or not parents *should* be educating their young about sex, the fact is that the great majority of them are still not doing so. When adolescents in a recent national survey in the United States were asked whether their parents talked 'pretty freely' about sex, over 70 per cent of both boys and girls, virgins and non-virgins, replied that they did not. When asked specifically if their parents had ever discussed such topics as masturbation, contraceptive methods, or venereal disease, two-thirds or more said they had not.[1]

The notion that adolescents have nothing left to learn about sex stands on equally flimsy ground. Myths are widespread (more than a quarter of adolescents 16 and over expressed the belief that 'if a girl doesn't want to have a baby, she won't get pregnant' even if she fails to use any contraceptive measure).

Nevertheless, only about a third of high schools in the United States provide comprehensive sex education.

Among adolescents themselves the great majority strongly favour sex education in schools and deny that it leads to greater sexual experimentation (they appear to be right: among American adolescents, fewer non-virgins than virgins have received adequate sex education).

Contemporary sexual attitudes and behaviour

One of the more prominent aspects of the youth culture of the 1960s—and clearly one of the more enduring—was the development of a 'new sexual morality'. This brought a greater openness and honesty about sex and an increasing tendency to see decisions about individual sexual behaviour as a purely private concern of the person or people involved.

To whatever degree society is 'permissive', the poignancy of young love is as unvarying and timeless as in the days of Aucussin and Nicolette.

This trend appears to reflect in part a growing disenchantment with established social institutions, together with a shift in values among many young people in the direction of self-discovery and self-expression—of 'doing one's own thing'. In a recent study, most adolescents in the sample agreed that 'it's right that people should make their own moral code', but only a minority (a quarter of 16- to 19-year-olds) agreed that 'so far as sex is concerned, I wouldn't do anything that society would disapprove of'.[2]

The growing emphasis on openness and honesty is not evidence of an increased preoccupation with sex, as many parents and other adults seem to think. Indeed, it may well be that today's average adolescent, accepting sex as a natural part of life, is less preoccupied and concerned with sex than his counterparts in earlier generations, with their atmosphere of secrecy, guilt and suppression. Most contemporary adolescents agree that 'my head is pretty well together as far as sex is concerned'; and over 80 per cent of all adolescents disagree with the notion that the most important thing in a love relationship is sex.[3]

Openness about sex means an adolescent attitude to pornography that may shock parents.

Changing values and sexual behaviour

How are these changing attitudes about sex among adolescents reflected in their behaviour? Although almost all adolescent boys already engaged in masturbation prior to the so-called 'youth revolution' of the sixties (and indeed did so as far back as human records go), there is some evidence that masturbation among boys is currently beginning at younger ages than in the past, and that this activity is accompanied by less anxiety and guilt than previously.[4] Among girls, recent data indicate that there has been a significant increase in the incidence of masturbation at all ages between 12 and 20. However, girls generally appear to engage in masturbation—or admit to it—only about half as often as boys. Interestingly, masturbation occurs about three times as frequently among those with experience of sexual intercourse or petting to orgasm as among the sexually inexperienced.

Petting appears to have increased somewhat in the past few decades, and it tends to occur earlier. The major change, however, has probably been in frequency of petting, degree of intimacy of the techniques involved, the frequency with which petting leads to erotic arousal or orgasm, and, certainly, frankness about this activity.

By 1973, for the first time, there were more non-virgins than virgins in the U.S. between 13 and 19 years old. And by the age of 16, almost half of the boys and a third of the girls had had sexual experience.[5]

These manifestations of sexuality—substitute activities—are something most societies and most parents have become used to dealing with. Currently, however, the greatest amount of parental and societal concern is focused on the dramatic increase in actual sexual intercourse among young people.

57

This trend has been found in the United States and other Western countries, although there are clear national differences in total incidence of premarital intercourse. For both males and females, England, West Germany and the Scandinavian countries (in that order) show a higher incidence than the United States and Canada, while some other countries, such as Ireland, show a lower incidence.[6]

But there are wide individual differences within each country, with the lowest incidence generally occurring among adolescents who are younger, female, highly religious, and politically conservative. More adolescent virgins than non-virgins have 'a lot of respect' for their parents' ideas and opinions, feel close to and liked by their parents, believe that their parents understand what they want out of life, and find it relatively easy to communicate with them. By contrast, nearly three times as many non-virgins as virgins agree that 'I've pretty much given up on ever being able to get along with my parents'. Compared with the parents of non-virgins, the parents of virgins are more likely to have discussed such topics as masturbation, birth control, venereal disease and sexual intercourse with their children.[7]

These findings are echoed in an investigation of American high school youth, where another important finding was that the degree of influence the mother had was related to the amount of maternal affection she exhibited. In other words, young people are more likely to fulfil parental expectations where the parental relationship itself is a loving and rewarding one.[8]

How parents would like adolescent sons to meet and treat girls . . .

Effects of the 'new morality'

In today's more open social climate, many experienced adolescents seem to be able to handle sexual involvement without undue stress. Four out of five non-virgins in the United States report getting 'a lot of satisfaction' out of their sex lives. Two-thirds of all non-virgins think that sex makes their lives 'more meaningful'.

However, significant minorities report feelings of guilt, find themselves exploited or rejected, or discover belatedly that they cannot cope emotionally with full sexual relationships. Especially after their first experience of intercourse, girls are far more likely than boys to experience negative feelings: whereas boys are most

... and how they fear they do meet them.

likely to report being excited, satisfied and happy, girls often report being afraid, guilty, worried, or embarrassed after their initiation. As one 16-year-old girl expressed it, 'I felt really guilty. I wondered if my mother really knew. When I came in after it happened, I felt I had guilt written all over my face'.

On the other hand, another 16-year-old girl who had been going with her boyfriend for several years, and was very much in love, had a very different experience: 'What were my feelings? . . . They were warm feelings, physically close feelings . . . The only thing I could think of is the wanting each other, a sharing each other. I still feel that way.'[9]

There are obvious dangers in the assumption that sexual involvement is 'OK as long as you're in love'. Encouraged by such a philosophy among peers, a girl or boy may become more deeply involved emotionally than she or he can handle responsibly at a particular stage of maturity. An adolescent may also think that his or her attitudes are more 'liberal' than they really are, and involvement may lead to unanticipated feelings of guilt, anxiety, or depression.

Psychologists who work with young people are also well aware that the motives for becoming involved in sexual activities are not always what they seem. In some cases the motivation has little to do with sex as such, or with maturity. Dr. Louis Fine, a paediatrician experienced in work with adolescents, has come to the conclusion that young people may become involved in sexual relationships not simply as the natural consequence of being 'in love', but as often to gain peer approval, to escape from or rebel against parents, to gain affection denied them by parents or others, or as a 'cry for help'.[10]

Pregnancy and contraception

Many girls today express the opinion that with the availability of 'the pill' they no longer have to be fearful of pregnancy: 'We just have to decide what is right.' Noble as this sentiment may be, the fact is that less than a third of unmarried girls having intercourse have used the contraceptive pill to prevent pregnancy. A disturbingly high percentage—between 55 and 75 per cent— have used no contraceptive device whatever, at least in their first experience. Only a minority consistently use such a device thereafter. Even among those in steady relationships, only two-thirds reported always using contraceptive devices.

This widespread failure to take contraceptive precautions, allied with the continuing increase in premarital intercourse among adolescents, has resulted in more than a million 15- to 19-year-old girls in the United States alone (10 per cent of this entire age group) becoming pregnant each year: two-thirds of these pregnancies are initiated out of wedlock. In addition, some 30,000 girls annually under the age of 15 become pregnant.[11]

The consequences of this 'epidemic' of adolescent pregnancies

Society does not smile on pregnant schoolgirls, however pleased they seem.

'If you can't stand the heat, get out of the kitchen'? No, these days you get out of your clothes!

are serious indeed. More than a quarter are terminated by induced abortion; 10 per cent result in marital births that were conceived premaritally; and over one-fifth result in out-of-wedlock births. Fourteen per cent simply miscarry. Even among the 27 per cent of adolescent pregnancies that occur post-maritally each year, problems are more frequent than among older women. Apart from the increased psychological and social difficulties of adolescent motherhood, adolescent pregnancies are more likely to endanger the physical health of both mother and child.

In recent surveys, the main reasons given for not using contraceptives were that the teenagers thought (usually mistakenly) that they could not become pregnant because of time of month, age or infrequency of intercourse; or because contraceptives were not available when they needed them. As the American Planned Parenthood Federation notes, 'The first set of reasons could be remedied with better education, the second with more adequate service programmes.' Yet only one in three high schools currently teach about birth control methods, despite the fact that eight out of 10 American adults old enough to have adolescent children favour such teaching.

Psychological studies have been carried out in several countries to compare sexually active adolescent girls who do and do not use contraceptives (or use them rarely). It has been found that those not using them tend often to hold fatalistic attitudes—to be more likely to feel powerless to control the events of their lives, to have a low sense of personal competence and to have a passive, dependent approach to male-female relationships. They are also more inclined generally to take risks, and to cope with anxiety by attempting to deny possible dangers rather than by facing up to them.[12] Some adolescents avoid contraceptive use because they fear it will spoil the 'spontaneity' of their relationships, or because they think it would indicate that they expected to have intercourse. This last reason is obviously based on shame. Another finding of these studies is that girls who accept their sexuality frankly are more likely to use contraceptives than those who deny it—whether to themselves or to others.

Only one in 15 pregnant adolescents stated that she did not use contraceptives because she was deliberately trying to have a baby. Only one in 11 indicated that she would not mind getting pregnant. However, among adolescents either seeking or not objecting to pregnancy, a common theme is that of emotional deprivation. In the words of one pregnant 15-year-old, 'For once in my life, I wanted to have something I could call my own, that I could love and that would love me.' Other related motivations may include 'being accepted as an adult', getting back at one's parents, 'holding' a boyfriend, gaining attention from peers, escaping school, or seeking change in a dull life.

It seems unlikely that there will be any reversal of the trend towards premarital intercourse as an accepted practice and towards the steady relationship as the most frequent and the most socially approved pattern among sexually experienced adolescents. What one must hope is that those adolescents who do enter sexual relationships can be helped to become sufficiently mature, informed, responsible, sure of their own identities and value systems, and sufficiently sensitive and concerned about the welfare of others, for the inevitable casualties of the 'sexual revolution' to be reduced to a minimum.

Whatever parents may have done in their own adolescences (and sexual experience among teenagers is no new phenomenon), whatever they may have felt about such relationships in their own 'pre-revolutionary' youth, it is vital for their own peace of mind and for the health of their relationships with their children to accept that, sooner or later, a son or daughter will be sexually involved with somebody else. That way 'casualties' can be avoided, the child may be spared the harrowing guilt and anxiety so frequent in the past, and growth towards maturity and emotional fulfilment encouraged rather than hindered.

Mixed messages: adolescents and masturbation

There are wide cultural differences in attitudes to masturbation, from harsh condemnation to complete tolerance. But in most Western countries, there has been a long history of strong disapproval, with the active support of religious groups and the medical profession. Even as late as the beginning of the present century, many physicians, including the Surgeon General of the United States, warned—and apparently believed—that masturbation weakened the individual and could cause a variety of diseases including cancer, heart disease, hysteria, impotence, frigidity, and even insanity. Despite such dire warning (for which there is no scientific basis whatsoever), most boys (and a considerable number of girls) continued to engage in this activity. It is not difficult to imagine the widespread anxiety, conflict, guilt, and depression suffered by many sensitive young people, sometimes for years. Some were even driven to suicide.

Although there has been a marked liberalisation of views in recent years among professionals, parents, and young people themselves, masturbation is still a source of concern for a significant number of adolescents. And there are still physicians who assert that masturbation among children or adolescents is likely to make it difficult for them later to transfer to heterosexual intercourse.

What are the facts? Obviously, early predictions that masturbation would severely impair physical and psychological health are wrong, inasmuch as, among boys at least, the practice has always been virtually universal and the world has gone on much the same. Furthermore, in the absence of previously acquired guilt or anxiety, masturbation may be both enjoyable and tension-reducing. There is no indication that it increases the difficulty of later adjustment to heterosexual relations—indeed, available evidence suggests the reverse may be the case.

In the case of women who have difficulty achieving orgasm during sexual intercourse, sex therapists have found that practice in masturbation can often be of help in learning sexual arousal during intercourse.[13] Alfred Kinsey, author of the famous Kinsey reports, found that women who had achieved orgasm through masturbation prior to marriage were more likely to achieve orgasm during intercourse in the first year of marriage.

It is sometimes argued that masturbation, though not physically harmful, may lead to a preoccupation with sex. It seems more reasonable to suppose that such preoccupation is likely to result from continuing, anxiety-ridden efforts to avoid masturbation, especially in the case of males. Nevertheless, in some instances masturbation may reflect adolescent adjustment problems. Young people who use masturbation not just as a sexual outlet when 'real' sex is unavailable but as a substitute for other activities in which they feel inadequate—whether involving peer-group projects or more individual pursuits—have a problem. So do those who engage in masturbation not in addition to or as a temporary substitute for 'real' sex but as a full replacement of—or refuge from—efforts to establish satisfactory relationships with opposite-sex peers.

Homosexual behaviour

Many adolescents worry at one time or another that they may be 'homosexual'. Because they have engaged in sexual activities with others of the same sex during pre-adolescence or adolescence, or thought of doing so, they think they must be 'queer'.

The fact is that at least half of all boys, and one-third of girls, have engaged in some form of sex play with other members of the same sex during pre-adolescence. Most of these young people go on to lead uncomplicated heterosexual lives. Some social critics claim that greater freedom of discussion about homosexuality and greater tolerance of homosexuals are leading to an increased number of persons with a primarily homosexual orientation; but in fact there has been little, if any, change in the past 30 years.[14]

For many young people, the rapid increase in sexual drive that accompanies puberty comes at a time when close social relationships and recreational activities are largely confined to members of the same sex. It is a period when the opposite sex still seems a bit strange and mysterious, and sometimes anxiety-producing. In their physical development, their changing sexuality and the feelings it elicits, and in their interests, younger adolescents are likely to have more in common with members of their own sex than with members of the opposite sex.

Proximity itself, plus a knowledge that others of the same sex are having the same kinds of sexual feelings and experiences, may lead to discussions about sex with the same-sex friends. It may subsequently lead to sexual experimentation, as in comparing sexual organs, masturbating in each other's presence, or mutual masturbation. Sometimes discussion of what sex with a member of the opposite sex must be like may lead to attempts to

imitate it as best one can without the complementary sexual equipment. Such 'homosexual' experiences often represent efforts to come to terms with, or better understand, one's own normal sexuality, rather than a strong or exclusive homosexual attraction.

A common experience among adolescent girls is a particularly warm, affectionate relationship with a special friend—the so-called schoolgirl crush. Such girls may spend hours together, sharing each other's dreams, hopes, and worries, and making elaborate plans for future activities. Partly because demonstrations of physical affection between girls are less frowned on than is the case with boys, and partly because girls generally are somewhat more oriented towards close emotional relationships, they may engage in affectionate hugging, kissing, holding hands, and the like. This activity may not be sexual at all. However, given the girls' newfound capacity for sexual responsiveness, it may sometimes shade over into pleasurable sexual stimulation— not infrequently to both girls' initial surprise.

It is also important to recognise that, despite popular notions to the contrary, heterosexuality and homosexuality are not either-or, mutually exclusive states. Kinsey found that most adults are more or less exclusively heterosexual. A small minority, probably no more than two to three per cent, are exclusively homosexual. But a quarter of adults fall in between these two groups. They may be mainly heterosexual, but with some homosexual involvement, or the reverse. Ten to 12 per cent of males, and half that proportion of females, have at least one homosexual experience after the age of 19. The most important factor in predicting whether an adolescent will become primarily or exclusively homosexual in orientation is not whether the young person is capable of sexual arousal with members of the same sex, but whether he or she is incapable, for whatever reason or reasons, of attraction to the opposite sex.

Homosexuality once aroused horrified revulsion: now it is a tolerated aspect of society in both women and men.

By teasing boys about their early, sometimes awkward attempts at establishing relationships with girls, by giving girls the impression that relationships with boys are something to be fearful about, or by implying to both boys and girls that sex itself is something furtive, dirty, or best not talked about, parents may increase the likelihood of homosexual involvement.

What about 'true' homosexuality?

Although most adolescents who have had homosexual experiences adopt a heterosexual life style, some—a minority—do not. We still lack a clear understanding of why this happens. In some instances, disturbed parent-child relationships seem to play a part. Homosexuality seems to occur more frequently among boys with overly intrusive, dominating mothers and detached or rejecting fathers.

Among girls, a number of factors may contribute to a homosexual orientation: a sexual education that encourages girls to view men as dangerous, threatening, or dirty, or, conversely, as weak and inadequate; or the situation in which the father,

while outwardly puritanical, is subtly seductive, encouraging a too-close relationship with himself but discouraging relationships with boys who are the girl's own age—a parallel to the overly intimate, close-binding mother in the case of males.

However, we also find heterosexual males and females who seem to have survived such distorted parental relationships, and homosexuals who appear to have had basically normal interactions with their parents. Attempts to find a physiological basis for homosexuality have so far been largely unproductive, although it has been suggested that chromosomal or hormonal anomalies or other biological conditions may accompany it.

Faced with a genuinely homosexual son or daughter, parents need above all to maintain a sense of perspective. There can be little argument with the fact that, in general in our society, homosexuals are likely to face a more difficult life than heterosexuals. Despite recent trends towards greater tolerance, they will encounter more discrimination, more hostility, more difficulty in finding rewarding interpersonal and sexual relationships, less chance for parenthood, and more limited vocational opportunities in many occupations (although in some others they may well be more likely to succeed). These young people are therefore on the whole likely to need more understanding and support from those closest to them, not less.

Finally, the *quality* of one's relationships—whether one is warm, thoughtful, or considerate, rather than thoughtless, cold, or exploitative—is surely more important than whether one's sexual attractions are for the same or opposite sex.

Relationships are like cloth: 'Never mind the width, feel the quality.'

6 Adolescents and their peers

Peers—the contemporaries or age-mates with whom a young person spends much of his or her time—play a crucial role in the psychological and social development of most adolescents. This is especially so in age-segregated technological societies like our own, where entrance into the adult world of work and family responsibility is increasingly delayed.

Of course, peer influences do not begin in adolescence; but they are especially critical then. Relations with both same- and opposite-sex peers during the adolescent years come close to serving as prototypes for later adult relationships.

Adolescents are also more dependent on peer relationships than are younger children, simply because ties to parents become progressively looser as the adolescent gains greater independence. In addition, relations with family members are likely to become charged with conflicting emotions in the early years of adolescence—dependent yearnings existing alongside independent strivings, hostility mixed with love, and conflicts developing between intra-familial and external cultural values and social behaviour. Many areas of the adolescent's inner life and outward behaviour consequently become difficult to share with parents. Parents, in turn, having managed to repress many of the painful emotional ups and downs of their own adolescence, may have difficulty in understanding and sharing their adolescent children's problems, even though they make an effort to do so. They are beyond what may be seen on both sides as a barrier, no matter how benevolent the feelings between them may be.

Yet people need, in adolescence perhaps more than at any other time in their lives, to be able to share strong and often confusing emotions, doubts and dreams with others. 'Adolescence is generally a time of intense sociability, but it is also often a time of intense loneliness. Merely being with others does not solve the problem; frequently the young person may feel most alone in the midst of a crowd, at a party or a dance.'[1] This means that acceptance by peers generally, and especially having one or more close friends, may be of crucial importance in a young person's life. The role of the peer group in helping an individual to define his or her own identity is particularly important: at no other stage of development is the sense of identity so fluid.

Face to face with adolescence.

*A cohesive, exclusive,
age-limited 'set'—
which may not prepare
them very well for
a world where
all ages have to mix.*

Conformity with peers

Not surprisingly, the heightened importance of the peer group during adolescence leads to heightened needs to conform to its standards, behaviour, fads and fashions. Parents may wonder why it seems so important to their adolescent sons and daughters to have the specific brand of denim jeans currently in fashion, and no other, or why only certain kinds of music, hair styles, language, dances, foods, recreational activities, sports, hobbies, television programmes—the list goes on and on—are acceptable. To the parent, these passionate addictions, and the rapid shifts they undergo, may seem bewildering because they seem so arbitrary and trivial. But to the adolescent, for whom they serve as badges of belonging and an insurance policy for the future,

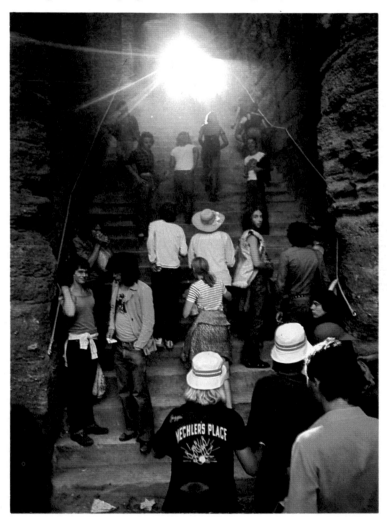

Contemporaneity imposes its own uniformity.

they are anything but trivial. They also serve another important purpose—to establish, at least superficially, a clear line of demarcation from adults. Adolescents with the world of childhood behind them and full adulthood still ahead, are virtually forced to create at least a semblance of an 'interim culture' of their own, clearly distinguishable from that of adults.

Parents should perhaps take comfort in these relatively harmless manifestations of difference. For if adolescents can satisfy their striving for independence and separate identity in these relatively superficial ways, they are less likely to express it in more fundamental and ultimately far more important matters, such as basic moral values and beliefs. Research has shown that where parents have a basically good relationship with their adolescent young, they usually have a stronger influence on the young person's basic values, beliefs, and life goals than do peers. Peers, on the other hand, play a stronger role in influencing current modes of social interaction, and tastes in dress, music, language, and the like.[2]

Crowds and cliques
The school-age child's world tends to be populated 'with friends, best friends and faceless strangers'.[3] The adolescent's circle of acquaintances is far wider: peer relationships generally fall within one of three categories: the broader 'crowd', the smaller, more intimate 'clique', and individual friendships. The crowd serves as the reservoir for larger, more organised social activities, while the more intimate and cohesive clique provides a source of security and companionship. In this small group, based on

Adolescent groups, far more than adults', tend to coalesce by reference to their interests.

mutual attraction, members can exchange information, discuss plans for crowd activities, and share some of their dreams, hopes, and worries—though not to the extent that close friends can. Girls' cliques tend to be relatively small and concerned more with interpersonal relationships: boys' cliques, or 'gangs', tend to be somewhat larger, less intimate, and more focused on shared activities such as sports and hobbies.

Friendships

Among the peer relationships of adolescents, friendships hold a special place. They are more intimate, involve more intense feelings, and are more honest and open than other relationships. There is less defensiveness, and less need for self-conscious attempts at role-playing in order to gain greater popularity and acceptance. In such relationships, 'There is trust, there is no need to pretend, no necessity for being on guard against betrayal of shared secrets.'[4]

Adolescents want friends to be loyal, trustworthy, and a reliable source of support in any emotional crisis. In the words of one 14-year-old urban black girl, 'A friend don't talk behind your back. If they are a true friend they help you get out of trouble and they will always be right behind you and they help you get through stuff. And they never snitch on you. That's what a friend is.'[5]

At their best, friendships may help young people to learn how to deal with their own complex feelings and those of others. They can serve as a kind of therapy by allowing the freer expression of otherwise suppressed feelings of anger or anxiety. They can also provide the priceless evidence that what one is going through as an adolescent is not unique.[6] As one 16-year-old expressed it, 'My best friend means a lot to me. We can talk about a lot of things I could never talk about with my parents or other kids— like hassles we're getting or problems we're worried about, and like ideals and things. It really helps to know you're not the only one that has things that bother them.'

Unfortunately the course of adolescent friendship does not always run smoothly. By virtue of their very intensity, such friendships may founder more easily than those of adulthood

Spurious categories: the 'fathers' race' brings together people with nothing in common but an incidental state.

(which usually involve more modest demands, but also yield more modest rewards). Young people with the greatest number of personal problems may have the greatest need for close friendships, but the least ability to sustain them and to avoid hurt feelings, suspicions, or recriminations. And even the most stable and rewarding of adolescent friendships is likely to blow hot and cold, if only because each of the parties to it is in a period of rapidly changing needs, feelings and problems, which in the nature of things will only rarely coincide. Parents sometimes find the adolescent's choice of friends incomprehensible. Although, in general, friends tend to similarity in social backgrounds,

Real categories: adolescents have a genuine identity of characteristics.

personalities, interests, and goals, an 'attraction of opposites' is by no means rare, usually because the young person finds in the friend some quality felt to be desirable but lacking in himself or herself.

Friendship patterns vary with age and sex
With the approach of the middle years of adolescence, friendships typically become more intimate, more emotionally interdependent, and more centred on the personalities of the participants than in earlier years.

Public togetherness...

...and private communion.

During this period, the opportunity for shared thoughts and feelings may help to ease the gradual transition to heterosexual relationships and a developing sense of one's own sex-role identity. It is also at this time that adolescent friendships, because of their very intensity, are most vulnerable to disruption. By contrast, in late adolescence friendships, even strong friendships, tend to be calmer, more equable, less exclusive, and more tolerant—in a word, more mature.

Within these general trends, there also tend to be sex differences in adolescent friendships. Girls' friendships are likely to be somewhat deeper, more open, more emotionally interdependent and more concerned with mutual support and encouragement. Boys seem to want a congenial companion with whom to share common interests, are more likely to be outwardly competitive, and less likely to offer physical demonstrations of affection, at least partly because of social taboos (although the habit of friends walking arm-in-arm or with arms round each other's shoulders persists in some strongly cohesive groups such as boarding-school inmates, and team-mates may hug one another on the sports field after some triumph).[7]

Social acceptance, neglect, and rejection

Because peers play such an important role in the lives of most adolescents, social acceptance is likely to be an urgent concern for most young people. Few adolescents—or adults—are immune to the effects of social neglect or rejection. A few rugged individualists, confident of their own goals and interests and possessed of a strong sense of their own identity, may neither need nor seek the approval of their peers. But most young people still judge their own worth to a considerable extent in terms of the way others react to them and remain dependent on the approval and acclaim of their peers.

Unfortunately, unpopular adolescents are likely to be caught in a vicious circle. If they are already emotionally troubled, self-preoccupied, and lack a secure concept of themselves, they are likely to meet with rejection or indifference from peers—which in turn further undermines self-confidence and increases the sense of social isolation. Other things being equal, social acceptance by the adolescent's peers is desirable—particularly if it is based on mutual helpfulness and shared interests. However, too great an emphasis, by parents or adolescents, on the pursuit of popularity—on 'fitting-in' in an organisation-minded society, rather than pursuing private, 'inner-directed' adolescent dreams and goals—simply invites the real pain of 'not belonging' when some setback occurs.

Boys and girls together

During pre-adolescence, boys tend to associate largely with boys, and girls with girls. There is a wariness towards the opposite sex that is at least partly self-protective and defensive, precluding,

Boy-games, girl-games in pre-adolescence— but a few years will make boy-and-girl games seem more important.

for example premature heterosexual relationships with which the emerging adolescent is unprepared to cope and which consequently may produce anxiety. It is not surprising to hear an 11-year-old boy describe girls as 'utter menaces' or to hear similar-age girls discuss boys as 'very stupid and not needed' or as 'something that kicks and punches'.[8]

As the young person enters adolescence, wariness of the opposite sex—or outright scorn—diminishes, and heterosexual interests increase. Nevertheless, boy-girl relationships in their early stages still reflect many pre-adolescent characteristics. Self-preoccupation and concern remain strong, deep emotional involvement is rare, and there is usually a superficial, gamelike quality to heterosexual interactions. At this stage, heterosexual group activities are common, and provide the security of having familiar members of the same sex present. Such activities allow the young person to discover ways of relating to the other sex without having to cope with being in one-to-one intimacy for prolonged periods.

Gradually the young person becomes more familiar with members of the opposite sex and more confident of his or her ability to relate to them. At the same time, increased personal maturity—less narcissism, a clearer sense of self, and a greater capacity to be concerned with others—is likely to lead to deeper and more meaningful relationships. At their best, such relationships include sexual attraction and social enjoyment, as well as feelings of mutual trust and confidence, a genuine sharing of interests, and a serious involvement in the well-being of the other partner to the relationship.

When allowed to develop at a pace that is natural and unforced for the particular boy or girl concerned, such relationships can play an important part in the growth towards maturity. Unfortunately, in a number of Western countries, and particularly in America, there are often artificial pressures to speed up this process and to encourage 'going steady' at ever younger ages.

In some cases, the pressure comes from peers. In other instances, however, it comes from parents, particularly those who are obsessed with their children's 'popularity' or with premature concerns about heterosexual development. A father may ask his 14-year-old son, 'Why do you spend all your time messing around playing baseball with other boys, or working on your radio set? Aren't you interested in girls?'

A 15-year-old girl recently told me, 'To listen to my mother, you'd think I'm already giving up the chance of ever getting married. When I tell her I'd rather spend an evening reading or talking to my girlfriends than go on a date with some boy I hardly know, you'd think it was the end of the world.'

The adolescent who begins restricting his or her relations to one member of the opposite sex at too early an age is likely to miss a number of important developmental experiences.

For one thing, he or she may never achieve the benefits of same-sex friendships discussed above (and such friendships can be very important in adult life, even after marriage). Furthermore, when young people begin 'going steady' at an age when both parties are still emotionally and socially immature, the relationship itself is likely to suffer these same drawbacks. Their further development into mature, self-reliant people in their own right may itself be jeopardised: they may tend to use their relationship as a way of avoiding other important developmental tasks. Finally, they may miss the invaluable opportunity adolescence provides of getting to know, understand, and enjoy a wide variety of acquaintances of both sexes—human beings in general rather than one idiosyncratic specimen in particular.

Research has shown that girls who begin dating very early (ages 11-14) and those who do not date at all—even in late adolescence—are both at a developmental disadvantage. Adolescent girls who begin dating early tend to be active, energetic and self-confident, but they are also immature, superficial, unimaginative, and limited in their interests and friendships, especially with other girls. Those who do not date at all tend to be retarded in social development, overly dependent on parents, insecure, and self-absorbed.[9] These personality characteristics are clearly not attributable solely to the dating pattern. Pre-existing personality characteristics are at least as likely to influence dating practices as the reverse. But once the pattern begins, a vicious circle appears to be set in motion, further reinforcing the girls' particular liabilities.

Adolescent marriage

Does the boy or girl who marries a high school sweetheart have a happier marriage than peers who do not? The answer is clearly no, on the whole, if they marry while both are still adolescents. The requirements of marriage in our society are complex and difficult to fulfil at any age, as a steadily mounting divorce rate makes painfully clear. And the burdens are likely to be considerably greater for married adolescents, who may still be struggling to complete their education, to establish themselves in a vocation, or simply to decide who they really are and what they want to be. Typically, married adolescents are also economically insecure or dependent on parents for financial assistance—either of which may create additional problems.

Adolescent marriages are often additionally complicated by the fact that they have resulted from pregnancy. According to one study, nearly three-quarters of premaritally pregnant brides were 18 or under; almost all were 21 or younger. A majority of 16-year-old girls and more than one-third of 17-year-olds who married were pregnant.[10] In such cases, the young people may not be marrying the person they would ultimately choose. Even if they are, they have less time to become adjusted to each other and to the demands of marriage before undertaking the responsibilities and restrictions of parenthood.

Consequently it is not surprising to find that in the first five years of marriage, the divorce rate of both men and women who married under the age of 20 is more than twice that of those married at later ages, and that the rate remains consistently higher throughout life. Furthermore, the younger the adolescent partners are when they marry, the greater is the likelihood of divorce or legal separation. This is not to say that adolescent marriages *cannot* be successful. With help and support from families, schools, and other social institutions, a significant number of such marriages do succeed, although the road is seldom easy.

7 Adolescents and drugs

Many adults believe that the marked increase in adolescent drug use during the past decade in the United States and other Western countries is a unique, isolated phenomenon. Such a view is misleading, and can only obstruct attempts to put the problem in its proper perspective. Widespread drug use and abuse are not restricted to adolescents, and did not begin with the advent of Sixties youth culture, as anybody who was 20 in the Twenties can testify.

Although there may be significant differences between generations in their patterns of drug use, the broader society of which adolescents are a part has been developing into a 'drug culture' for many years. For example, one-quarter to one-third of all prescriptions currently being written in the United States are for pep or diet pills (amphetamines) or tranquillisers. Between 1964 and 1977, prescriptions for Valium and Librium, the two most widely used tranquillisers, increased from 40 to 73 million a year in the United States alone.

Television and radio bombard viewers with insistent messages that relief for almost anything—anxiety, depression, restlessness —is 'just a swallow away'. In the words of one 13-year-old, 'We're not supposed to take drugs but TV is full of commercials showing people running for a pill because something is bugging them.' Adolescents who have adopted this view of how life is to be coped with may only be reflecting societal and parental models.

Research has shown that young people whose parents make significant use of such drugs as alcohol, tranquillisers, tobacco, sedatives and amphetamines are more likely than other adolescents to use marijuana, alcohol and other drugs themselves.[1] As one 15-year-old boy told me, 'In my house, you can't sneeze without getting a pill. My mother is always taking something for headaches and my father is always taking something to keep awake to get work done at night. They're not drunks but they sure drink a lot. So, now I'm a criminal for smoking pot?'

It is also true that while too many adolescents are becoming serious, high-risk drug users, the majority are not. Despite dire predictions in the late 1960s about the imminence of an 'epidemic'

*Puff the magic
drag in . . .*

Shooting it up ...

of adolescent drug use, nothing of the kind has materialised. Use of marijuana, alcohol, and tobacco is widespread among young people; but the use of 'counterculture' drugs such as LSD and similar substances, inhalants (as in 'glue sniffing'), 'uppers' (amphetamines) and 'downers' (barbiturates), and more recent entrants into the youthful drug scene such as heroin, cocaine, PCP ('Angel Dust'), Quaaludes and the like, has not been detected in more than one person in five in the United States (and is generally less in most other Western countries). Many former occasional users have given up such drugs without their places having been taken by younger recruits.

Nevertheless, there is no room for complacency. Although it is accurate, for example, to state that 'only' 3 to 5 per cent of junior and senior high school students in the United States have ever tried heroin, this still adds up to over a million young people. In addition, use of 'traditional' (i.e. adult) drugs, particularly alcohol, has increased in recent years, most dramatically among younger adolescents. (For an account of the different drugs in use today, their history and their effects, including alcohol and nicotine, see *Addictions* by Jerome Jaffe, Bob Petersen and Ray Hodgson in this series.)

Alcohol

A common refrain among many parents of adolescents today is: 'I'm becoming concerned about his (or her) drinking, but at least it's better than drugs.' In fact, however, alcohol is just as much a psychoactive drug as, say, marijuana, and its dangers have been far more clearly established by scientists and physicians. Furthermore, the use of alcohol is more common among marijuana and other drug users than among non-users of such 'untraditional' drugs.

Most adolescents have at least tried alcoholic beverages at some time, although the frequency of use varies with age, sex, religion, social class, place of residence and country of origin. In most countries outside the Muslim lands, alcohol is the most frequently used of all psychoactive drugs, including marijuana. It is estimated that in the United States between 71 and 92 per cent of adolescents have tried alcohol by the end of the teenage years. It should be noted, however, that most adolescents who have engaged in drinking are temperate in their use of alcohol, and are likely to remain so.

... and knocking it back. Alcohol is as much a 'drug' as is heroin.

Nevertheless, if one uses getting high or drunk once a week or more as a criterion of problem drinking, about 5 per cent of United States teenagers at high school are already problem drinkers.[2] And these figures only include students still in school. It is known that problem drinking is higher among school dropouts, and that adolescents are beginning to drink, and are drinking more, at ever younger ages.

Marijuana

Among adolescents who have experimented with one or another illicit drug, marijuana users account for by far the greatest percentage. In the United States currently, more than half of all young people have at least experimented with marijuana.

79

Most users are experimenters and occasional, moderate smokers, and do not differ greatly from non-users in emotional adjustment. It is only among chronic heavy users that there are fairly consistent indications of real psychological and social disturbance, as distinguished from simple differences in personality or lifestyle. However, since heavy chronic marijuana use is typically associated with multiple use of other drugs, a direct cause-effect relationship between heavy use and emotional disturbance is difficult to establish. Furthermore, studies of multiple drug users suggest that heavy drug use is primarily a result of psychological and social disturbance, rather than its cause. Obviously, once such drug use has begun, a 'vicious circle' may be initiated with mutual reinforcement of both disturbance and drug need.[3]

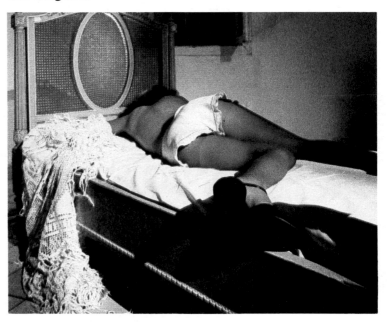

The search for a 'high' can lead to oblivion.

Why do adolescents take drugs?

One reason why adolescents may try a drug is simply that it is there. Our society has, to a large extent, become a 'drug culture': unlike the average young person of fifty years ago, whose opportunities for drug use were limited in most countries to alcohol and tobacco, today's adolescent faces a cornucopia of drugs from which to choose, both those sold in pharmacies and those available only on the street. Adolescents are characteristically curious about their expanding world, and far more inclined than most adults to take risks. This is probably partly to prove their boldness—'not being chicken'—and their sense of adventure, and partly because they do not believe, at least initially, that anything disastrous can happen to *them*. Thus, for many adolescents, some experimenting with drugs may take place simply out of curiosity, a sense of daring, and opportunity. In limited amounts, some drug use—an occasional marijuana cigarette, or as older adults may more readily recognise, an occasional social cocktail—can be 'fun'. But this is not to say it is desirable.

Peer group influences

Young people may also try drugs because of peer group influences—a need to be accepted by a group of peers who are already involved with drugs. In recent research, it has been found

Is this addiction, rebellion—or only a badge of 'belonging'?

that one of the best predictors of whether an adolescent will become involved with a drug is use of that drug by friends, especially the young person's 'best friend'. Adolescents themselves acknowledge the importance of peer group influences.

Other young people may experiment with drugs to please a special boyfriend or girlfriend. This appeared to be the case with a 14-year-old California girl: 'I smoked pot with my boyfriend and then he wanted to try LSD. I was scared but he told me that if I didn't go along with him, he'd find a girl who would.'[4]

Rebellion against parents

All adolescents, at one time or another, need to assert their independence from their parents. But whether their rebelliousness will take the form of *serious* drug use appears to depend a good deal on the kind of relationships the adolescent has had with his or her parents. For the child of democratic, authoritative, loving parents (especially those with relatively traditional values), who allow their children gradually increasing, age-appropriate opportunities to 'test their wings', the risk of serious drug involvement is generally lower than that for the child whose parents have not been loving, and who are neglectful, overly permissive, or—in contrast—authoritarian and hostile.

81

Hubble-bubble
Bringing trouble:
Eyes on fire,
Seeing double.

One angry adolescent said of his parents: 'They're always telling me what to do, like I don't have any mind of my own. And like my father is sitting around having his third Martini before supper, and telling me like he's some big expert, and I'm an idiot, about how marijuana will destroy my brain. Well, the hell with him.'

An adolescent girl, on the other hand, seemed mostly to be trying to get some response—any response—from her parents as a sign that they cared: 'I've been on drugs since I was twelve. My parents think I'm rebelling about something, but they don't know what. It's them. Not that they're strict. It's just that they're not really there and you feel you have to jump up and down and scream before they really notice.'[5]

Escape from the pressures of life

Another reason for drug use, often given by adolescents themselves, is escape from tension and the pressures of life, or from boredom. Ironically, this is also a major reason why adults use drugs like alcohol and barbiturates. Indeed, one of the greatest dangers of drug use by adolescents is that it can become a substitute for learning to deal with the daily problems and inevitable frustrations of living. As the former director of the National Institute of Mental Health in the United States has stated: 'Patterns of coping with reality developed during the teenage period are significant in determining adult behaviour. Persistent use of an agent which serves to ward off reality during this critical developmental period is likely to compromise seriously the future ability of the individual to make an adequate adjustment to a complex society.'[6]

Alienation

Some adolescent drug use may reflect alienation—a profound rejection of the values of an adult society that some young people perceive as increasingly impersonal, often cruel, and lacking in concern for the individual. This was often the case during the troubled decade of the 1960s, particularly in America. A significant minority of adolescents and youth renounced the 'rewards' of organised society and turned inwards to the self-preoccupied world of mind-altering drugs (conspicuously, marijuana and the 'psychedelic' drugs, such as LSD, mescalin, and peyote) in order—mistakenly or not—to seek a renewal of wonder, trust, beauty and meaning.

Emotional disturbance.

For other young people, particularly heavy multiple drug users, reliance on drugs may reflect emotional disturbances of varying degrees of severity, and an inability to cope with the demands of living or to find a meaningful personal identity. In some cases, we need to look to profound disturbances in family relationships during the course of development for clues to the young person's difficulties. Among adolescents in residential treatment centres and half-way houses for alcohol and drug users (usually in combination), common themes acknowledged both by the staff and recovering users were feelings of parental rejection or indifference; lack of acceptance by peers; emotional isolation; and low self-esteem, which they felt a need to conceal behind a defence of 'appearing cool'.

Some young people who have been using alcohol or drugs steadily since pre-adolescence acknowledge that they have never known any other way to cope with anxiety, boredom, depression, fear of failure, or lack of purpose. Poignantly, an important aim

Day out for one kind of tripper: society disapproves.

of one treatment programme—in addition to helping young people to learn to deal with their personal problems and establish genuine friendships with peers—was simply to teach them how to have fun without drugs!

What can parents do?

What can parents do to keep their sons and daughters from becoming seriously involved with drugs, or to deal with the problem if it occurs? Obviously, of the two, prevention is the more desirable alternative. But even the most enlightened, sensible parents cannot guarantee that their children will not become involved with some drug experimentation. This is especially likely to happen in communities where drug use is prevalent, and where there are strong peer pressures on the adolescent to participate.

There are, however, a number of steps that parents can take to minimise the likelihood of adolescent drug use, or to limit its seriousness should it occur. First and foremost, parents should try to keep open the lines of communication with their children. They can talk to them (not at them); they can listen to them, they can encourage them to speak frankly, even when there is a good chance that their views will differ.

Secondly, they can help their children to begin learning to become more independent and to take increasing responsibility for their own actions long before the onset of adolescence. Parents who think that they can continue—sometime indefinitely—to run the lives of their adolescent young and protect them from any adverse consequences of their actions are not preparing them for coping with exposure to drugs—or indeed with life itself.

Parents also need to remember that they are role models.

Day out for another kind of tripper: society approves.

Children take their cues from what parents do as well as from what they say. If parents present models of stable, responsible behaviour, facing their problems in a realistic way, their young are likely to do the same. On the other hand, if parents are indecisive, avoid taking responsibility, or attempt to rationalise problems away, their sons and daughters will get the message just as loudly and clearly.

If their parents use drugs rarely, and only for responsible, well defined purposes, adolescents are much more likely to do the same than if their parents are forever running from one drug to another—to sleep, to stay awake, to relax, to cope with anxiety or pressure, or to 'pick up their spirits'. Even where parents are struggling with a drug problem themselves, however, they can help the adolescent to avoid a similar predicament by being honest and open and admitting the difficulty they are having, rather than by denying the problem or attempting to rationalise it away. It is important for young people to know that their parents have basic values, and that they are making a real effort to live by them. The fact that the young person disagrees with some of these values is far less important than the knowledge that the values exist. In the end, this knowledge provides young people with a sense of trust and security, encourages them to think seriously about their own basic values and promotes respect for parents and a willingness to listen to their views.

Finally, adolescents need to know that their parents really care about them, not just in the abstract but in concrete, demonstrated ways: by shared family activities, and by knowing about and taking an interest in their children's schoolwork, hobbies, friends, social life, goals and dreams. None of these parental efforts can guarantee that a young person will not become involved in drug experimentation. But they can do much to lessen its likelihood, and to minimise the seriousness of the adolescent's drug use should it occur.

What if parents discover drug use?
If parents do find out that an adolescent has become involved with drugs, the most important initial advice is: 'don't panic'. Parents should first attempt to find out how serious the matter is. The average young person who has smoked a few joints or had a few drinks at a party is not in imminent danger of a trip down the road to oblivion, and by acting as if he or she were in danger, parents are likely only to aggravate any problem that exists and lessen the chances of communicating with and influencing the young person.

Assuming that the use of drugs is not, at least as yet, out of hand, parents should attempt to discover what lies behind it: curiosity, adventure, a simple desire to share in peer group activities; or resentment against parents, fear of school failure, deep feelings of inadequacy and low self-esteem, depression, or acute anxiety? Parents should attempt not only to talk to their children, but to look at the young person's life as a whole—and at themselves. Are they part of the problem, as well as part of the solution?

In many instances, honest efforts to explore these issues with a young person will greatly help in resolving the problem. If these efforts are to be successful, however, parents must know what they are talking about when discussing drugs, and they must be honest with the adolescent. They should be open and straightforward about their own values, beliefs, and concerns. At the same time, they should not let disagreement with or disapproval of the behaviour be construed as rejection of the person: 'hate the sin, but love the sinner'.

If such efforts fail, or if it becomes obvious that the adolescent's drug use has already become a serious, incapacitating problem, professional help should be sought promptly. But it should be made clear that this course is being taken not as punishment or out of anger but because of genuine caring and concern.

8 Moral growth and alienation

At no time in life is a person as likely to be concerned with moral values—with what is right and true, wrong or false—as during adolescence. Often for the first time in their lives, many young people become seriously troubled by questions about the existence of God, the injustice of the world, the morality of war and so on, as well as about more immediate topics (should one tell 'white lies'? or 'squeal' to authority about someone who cheats? or sleep with one's current 'date'?).

With the beginning of adolescence many young people— particularly the brighter and more sophisticated—may no longer be able to adopt without question the social, political, or religious beliefs of their parents. No longer do they believe that, solely because parents have particular beliefs, all right-thinking persons must necessarily share them. The adolescent is more able to think relatively, to see that perfectly honourable people may hold strongly opposed views.

The young person at this stage of development is also able to take motivation into account—to see that it is not simply a particular action that is good or bad, but also the intention of the person who takes the action.

With the newfound ability to think more abstractly, the adolescent is also likely to seek out broad moral principles that can be proposed as 'universally' true and can be applied regardless of the immediate circumstances, and regardless of whether they are 'popular'.

Changing social demands

Apart from increased mental sophistication there is another reason for the greater preoccupation of adolescents with problems of moral values, and this is the changing nature of the social demands that they face. The younger child lives in a narrower world than the adolescent, where the rules are mostly set by parents. But the adolescent boy or girl *must* make choices. Not only are adolescents changing, but their social world and their

*'I'm going to be
different—even if
it kills me!'*

87

relations with it are changing too: they are confronted with multiplying choices about ways to live their lives, only one of which can be plumped for at any one time. You cannot have your cake and eat it.

As adolescents develop cognitively, their time perspective extends further into the future. This, too, increases the feeling that developing a set of values is a matter of urgency. 'The young person who is beginning to look forward to an entire lifetime is much more in need of a set of guiding moral principles—if his or her life is to have a semblance of order, consistency, and meaning—than the child whose principal preoccupation at a given moment may be whether he is going to an amusement park the next day or to the dentist.'[1]

Adolescents are also subject to more conflicting values than are most younger children. Peers may be urging one set of values

Centres of attention: play ...

and parents another. And peers themselves may be divided in their values. One important group of friends and acquaintances may be telling the young person that there's nothing wrong with premarital sex or use of marijuana or alcohol; another group may have their doubts, or be opposed. Some peers may condone cheating in school; others may condemn it. Increasingly, other influences also enter the adolescent's arena of moral choice—teachers, movies, books, television, and representatives of conflicting groups in the broader society.

Conflicting pressures on adolescents with respect to moral values are not new, but their intensity has increased in recent years. A rapidly changing, complex adult society has become increasingly uncertain of its own purposes, and divisions of opinion regarding values have increased about such matters as

...and work.

sex, violence, censorship, women's aspirations, race. Such divisions have tended to make the transition from a 'father knows best' sort of moral thinking to a more independent approach harder than in earlier, simpler eras. Rapid social change and conflicting societal values also appear to have increased the danger, at least for a minority of young people, of falling into an extreme, essentially directionless and sometimes chronic kind of moral relativism at this critical juncture in their development. For such an adolescent, the idea that nothing is better, or worse, than anything else increases the likelihood of identity confusion.

Moral values and psychological conflicts

It is important to realise that, for many adolescents, the need to wrestle with broad questions of moral values is not always simply a result of concern with the issues for their own sake. Often, passionate but apparently abstract philosophical debates about such momentous issues as war and peace, or whether humans are basically aggressive or co-operative, may reflect an adolescent's concern—often unconscious—about being able to handle an increase in the strength of aggressive and rebellious impulses that is likely to accompany the onset of puberty, particularly in boys. Similarly, a girl may develop a highly intellectualised philosophy of free love, or become a vigorous crusader against traditional middle-class values, principally as a way of reassuring herself that she does not feel guilty about her own sexual impulses. Supposedly objective differences with parents about moral or political values and beliefs may more truly reflect efforts to establish an independent identity of one's own, or to express a deep resentment towards hostile or indifferent parents.

89

'The proof of the pudding is in the eating'

There is another side to the broad issue of moral development. This is the extent to which, and the manner in which, cognitive understanding is reflected in behaviour. A person may be able to think about moral issues with considerable sophistication and to formulate the proper moral course to take; but he or she may not always act in accordance with this formulation. In one study, children and adolescents were asked 'Why should people follow rules?' They were then asked, 'Why do *you* follow rules?'[2] In

Topless waitresses start here . . .

response to this second question, most middle-school children and adolescents showed a shift towards earlier, more 'primitive' levels. Despite the fact that they were mentally capable of understanding loftier reasons—such as 'to make things work better and to be fair to everybody'—they did not apply them to themselves. For example, although only 3 per cent of older adolescents said that people *should* follow rules simply 'to avoid negative consequences', 25 per cent said that they personally *would* do so for that reason. Some adolescents may show a reasonable degree of adherence to personal moral principles, even under considerable stress. Others may yield rather quickly to temptation or to group pressure. Still others may appear to be guided almost solely by the possibility of getting into trouble or losing some privilege, rather than by internalised moral standards of what is right. In short, knowledge alone, even sophisticated knowledge of moral standards, does not guarantee an effective conscience.

Parent power

What determines whether an adolescent is likely to have an effective conscience that serves as a strong guide to behaviour, even in the face of conflicting pressures? Many factors play a part, including social and peer group pressures, but probably the most important single factor is the role played by parents.

Even a crystal ball will not show how a child will turn out—but a mother's behaviour gives a clue.

Martin Hoffman, a psychologist at the University of Michigan, has found that there are two basic patterns of parental discipline that have different effects on moral development.[3] He calls them *power-assertive* and *non-power-assertive*. The second pattern can

be divided into two main sub-types: *love-withdrawal techniques* and *induction* (in which the parent provides explanations or reasons for requiring certain behaviours from the child).

In power-assertive techniques the parent does not rely on the child's own inner resources—such as guilt, shame, dependency, love, or respect—or provide the child with the relevant information needed to develop such resources in order to influence his or her behaviour. Instead the parent seeks to accomplish this by punishing the child physically or materially, or by relying on fear of punishment. Power assertion tends to be 'associated with weak moral development to a highly consistent degree'.[4] The child or adolescent is less likely to act on the basis of his or her own internalised moral norms—that is, conscience—and more likely to continue to be influenced by external rewards and punishments. Not surprisingly, a pattern of 'power assertion' is frequently found among the parents of some kinds of delinquents.

The parent who employs love-withdrawal techniques does not physically punish or deprive the child. Instead, he or she reacts to undesirable behaviour by such things as conspicuously ignoring the child, refusing to speak to him, expressing dislike, or even, in some cases, threatening to leave him. The message the child or adolescent gets is clear: 'if you behave this way, I won't love you'.

In fact, the implication is likely to be that the child is unlovable. As Professor Hoffman observes, although love-withdrawal does not involve physical or material threats, 'it may be more devastating emotionally than power assertion because it poses the ultimate threat of abandonment or separation'.[5] Love withdrawal also contributes little to the child's development of positive, mature, internalised moral standards, although he or she, motivated largely by anxiety, is more likely than the child of power-assertive parents to confess to violations and to accept blame. Furthermore, love withdrawal disrupts communication, and hence learning opportunities, between parent and child. It also fails to make use of the child's capacity for empathy.

There is, however, a third approach to parental discipline that *does* encourage the development of a mature conscience, based on internalised moral standards. It involves what Professor Hoffman calls *induction*. In this approach, the parent treats the child as a potentially responsible, capable individual. Such a parent explains to the child the reasons for requiring certain behaviours, and points out the practical realities of a situation, or how inappropriate behaviour may be harmful to the child or to others.

. . . awe-inspiring power.

Parents do not need to be saints to use inductive techniques. For example, mother can explain that if the child persists in some undesirable behaviour, it will worry her or wear her out, and consequently she will be likely to become irritable and cross with the child—and she does not want that to happen. In brief, she

93

can label the behaviour as 'unlovable'. But that is a far cry from labelling the child as unlovable.

Inductive techniques promote a positive identification with the parent, who is perceived as rational, reasonable, and non-arbitrary, and tend to foster the development of similar behaviour—and a mature conscience—in the child.

Alienation

Most adolescents eventually grow into reasonably happy, effective adults. But there remain large numbers of young people who do not; they feel deeply dissatisfied with the state of society, or themselves, or both. In the popular parlance of the 1960s and its youthful 'counterculture', these are young people who have become 'alienated'. The sources of their alienation, however, may vary widely. In some cases, the alienation results from economic deprivation or ethnic discrimination. Children can hardly be expected to identify with a society that has never given them anything but the crumbs from its table or the contempt of its privileged members. Such alienation will persist if the society

Adolescent alienation can manifest itself in lonely melancholy . . .

persists unchanged. In other cases, youthful alienation does not stem from personal disenfranchisement but from disillusion with a society that is viewed as pursuing goals of technological progress and economic affluence without regard to either the human or environmental costs. This sort of alienation characterised many middle and upper class youths in the late 1960s and early 1970s.

They also viewed the impersonal, highly specialised, status-oriented, hierarchical organisations of contemporary society (big business, government, education, the military) as inimical to values they held strongly. Particularly among American youth, the destructive, highly disruptive war in Vietnam was for many the culmination of their bitterness and disillusionment.[6] It was largely from alienated middle class youth of this period that the members of today's radical groups in such countries as Germany, Italy, Japan and the United States were recruited.

In still other cases, the roots of a young person's alienation lie primarily in disturbed parent-child relationships or other adverse developmental experiences; experiences that would be likely to produce psychological disturbance and a sense of alienation in almost any kind of society.

Young people can and do respond to their alienation in a variety of ways—some positive, some negative. Some find other, more personally meaningful ways of life, whether in social action (as in the case of work with children, the poor, the handicapped, or the elderly), in the pursuit of private goals (like some young artists, poets and craft workers), or in a community of like-minded souls (as in the case of some rural or urban communes or religious cults).

Others become social dropouts like the 'hippies' of the late 1960s and early 1970s, excessive drug users, delinquents, or political revolutionaries whose nihilistic aim may be simply the destruction of a society they despise. And some may develop serious psychological problems, as we shall see in the following chapter.

... or contemptuous hostility.

9 Psychological problems

Every young person will encounter some psychological problems in the course of growing up. No life can be, or indeed should be, totally free of anxiety, frustration, or conflict; like joy and love, these experiences are part of being human, and without them a life will lack its proper depth. Inescapably, such problems tend to crop up more frequently during periods of rapid developmental change and social transition— the beginning of school, the adjustment to adolescence.

An adolescent may have emotional ups and downs, periods of discouragement and worries about being accepted by peers. He or she may experience anxiety before an important examination, occasional outbursts of anger or rebellion, involvement with others in a minor delinquent act, sadness at the loss of a boyfriend or girlfriend, concerns about sex, or questions about his or her 'true' identity.

But this does not mean that the young person is psychologically disturbed or needs help other than normal parental understanding and support. It is only when such conditions are exaggerated, or threaten to become chronic, that it makes sense to talk of a clinically significant psychological disturbance and to seek professional help.

In this chapter, I shall briefly discuss a few of the more common, or more important, psychological disturbances that may be—not, let me emphasise, 'are likely to be'—encountered in adolescence.

The nature of symptoms

Some psychological problems are relatively easily understood. An adolescent girl who is constantly rejected by peers may become anxious and withdraw into lonely isolation. A boy who has been subjected to harsh or inconsistent discipline and to rejection or ridicule by his parents in the course of growing up may emerge as an angry and destructive adolescent. Other kinds of symptoms, however, are more puzzling—the suicide attempt that seems, at least on the surface, to have resulted from a relatively minor disappointment; acute anxiety, or even panic,

What may be only a time for reflection to an adolescent can look like dangerous brooding to adults.

that seems to have no identifiable source; an unrealistic fear of being alone, or of leaving the house. Many such seemingly mysterious or illogical symptoms have their source in, and act as a defence against, adolescent anxiety that may or may not be identified and acknowledged by those suffering from it—fear of loss of love; of angry, hostile feelings; of sexual impulses; or of personal inadequacy.

Sometimes these defences work—at least to some degree. An admittedly unrealistic fear (phobia) of leaving the house, for example, *may* help to conceal a deeper, unconscious fear of personal inability to cope with other people or with the demands of living. Fears such as this would be painful and anxiety-producing to admit consciously to oneself. But in some cases psychological defences are ineffective or only partly effective, and generalised or 'free-floating' anxiety may result.

Anxiety reactions

Anxiety reactions are unlike either normal fears (of realistically dangerous situations) or phobias (unrealistic fears) in that they may occur under any circumstances and are not restricted to specific situations or objects. The young person with an acute anxiety reaction feels a sudden fearfulness as if something bad were about to happen. He or she may become agitated and restless, startle easily, and complain of symptoms like dizziness or headache (which are often psychosomatic—real enough to the sufferer but without any organic cause). The ability to concentrate and pay attention may be limited, and the young person may appear distracted. Sleep disturbances are common.

Someone suffering from an acute anxiety reaction may be puzzled or alarmed about its apparently mysterious source, or may attribute it to a wide variety of isolated, and usually irrelevant, external circumstances or incidents.[1] On more careful inquiry, however, it usually becomes clear that far more extensive and more fundamental factors are involved—disturbed parent-child relationships, concerns about the demands of growing up, pervasive fears and guilt regarding sexuality, or aggressive impulses—although the adolescent may not be consciously aware of their role in the disturbance.

It is obviously essential to begin therapeutic intervention early once the anxiety reaction has been identified, so that the relevance of these causative factors can be more readily determined and dealt with. Treatment should begin before the onset of habitual or chronic anxiety and the beginning of a patterned response to it such as psychological withdrawal, impairment of school work, continuing physical symptoms or pains, diarrhoea, shortness of breath, fatigue, and the like.

Phobias

An intense fear which the individual consciously recognises as unrealistic is called a *phobia*. When unable to avoid or escape the phobic situation, a person may become extremely apprehensive and experience faintness, fatigue, palpitations, perspiration, nausea, tremor, and even panic. How can phobias be explained? In general, they can result from fear of some person, object, or event that is too painful and anxiety-producing to be allowed conscious awareness. Such a fear is displaced on to some other less unacceptable object or situation, usually one that is in some way symbolic of the original fear (in one case, for example it was eventually learned that a boy's intense fear of automobiles symbolically represented a strong fear of his father).

Unlike realistic fears, unrealistic or symbolic fears can best be ameliorated by attacking the *actual source* of the fear. It may also be helpful to *desensitise* (that is, gradually accustom) the individual to the displaced fear, if the phobia is of long standing.

School phobias

School phobia—a fear, which may approach panic, of leaving home and going to school—should not be confused with the occasional mild reluctance to go to school seen in normal children and adolescents, nor with realistic fears of going to school based, for example, on the expectation of bullying or abusive treatment by a particular teacher. Although many deeper problems may be unconsciously symbolised by a school phobia, it usually indicates a dread of some aspect of the school situation, concern with leaving home, or frequently both together.[2]

Leaving home, fearing school, both cause school phobia.

For example, a young person who remains overly dependent and is uncertain about his or her sexual identity, or who has fears of heterosexual relationships, may become acutely anxious in school when peers begin to organise their school life around dating, parties, and other heterosexual relationships. Adolescents in whose school phobia a prominent part is played by worries about leaving home (separation anxiety) are frequently excessively dependent. The dependence may be reinforced by overprotective behaviour by the child's mother.

Forcing a child or adolescent with a true, intense school phobia back into the dreaded situation will only aggravate matters. Prompt therapy—involving parents as well as the child—to determine and deal with the real source of the young person's anxiety is essential.

Just 'looking glum' should not be mistaken for depression.

Depression in adolescence

Saying that a person is 'depressed' tells us little. Depressive conditions may range from relatively undamaging, although acute, temporary states of sadness in response to a genuine loss (of a loved person, say, or of a settled relationship) to severely disturbed *psychotic* conditions that involve mental as well as emotional impairment. Such psychotic depressive disorders are rare in adolescence but depressed feelings on a less alarming scale are common. Indeed, as Irene Josselyn, an authority in the treatment of adolescents, asserts: 'If there is any emotional state that is universal for this age group it is depression.'[3]

For most adolescents such feelings are transient, a part of the emotional ups and downs that are frequent in adolescents. For some, however, depression or melancholy may become the dominant mood; it is at this point that it assumes the proportions of a true clinical disturbance requiring professional help. Left untreated, such depression may become chronic, and may even result in suicide.

Depression in adolescents usually manifests itself in a different way from that commonly encountered in depressed adults. They may be unwilling to talk about their feelings, and they may exhibit 'depressive equivalents' such as boredom or restlessness, which confuse the picture. An inability to be alone or a constant search for new activities, drugs, sexual promiscuity, delinquency, risk-taking (including, commonly, reckless driving), may all be indications of hidden depression, although obviously they may also be the result of other problems.

In general, adolescent depression is most likely to take one of two forms. In the first, the young person may complain of a lack of feelings and a sense of emptiness. It is a kind of depression resembling mourning: 'Adolescents of this group mourn for their childhood identity and cannot find an adult identity to which they can be wedded.'[4] It is not so much that the adolescent has no feelings as that he is sadly unable to deal with or express those he has.

A second type of adolescent depression is usually more difficult to resolve. It has its basis in longstanding, repeated experiences of defeat or failure. A large number of adolescent suicidal

Introspective boredom, persistent isolation, may be 'depressive equivalents'—and real danger signs.

attempts are not in fact the result of a momentary impulse, but of a long series of unsuccessful attempts to find alternative solutions to the young person's difficulties. The last straw in this type of depression is often the loss of a desired relationship, whether with a parent, friend or loved one.

Suicide

Suicide is rare in children. But from about the age of 15, the reported rate of suicide increases rapidly. In the United States alone, more than 4,000 young people between the ages of 15 and 24 are reported as suicides each year, and the rate has nearly tripled since the 1950s. Although this represents only a small proportion of the total population of adolescents and young adults, suicides are the third leading cause of death in this age group, exceeded only by accidents and homicides. Many more actual suicides are either undetected (as in the case of some fatal car accidents) or not reported as suicides.

In addition, the rate of suicide attempts is far higher than that of completed suicides—some experts estimate as much as 50 to 100 times higher. That would mean that in the United States alone as many as 200,000 to 400,000 young people may attempt suicide each year. Although adolescent boys outnumber girls in *completed* suicides, *attempted* suicides are far more common among girls. Most young people have a friend or acquaintance who has at some time attempted suicide.

But no absolute distinction can be made between actual and attempted suicides. In some cases what was intended, at least partly, simply as a gesture may backfire and lead to death. This is supposed to have happened in the tragic case of the brilliant young poet, Sylvia Plath, who turned on the gas in her house knowing that a babysitter was due to arrive soon. She even left a note about how to reach her doctor. Unfortunately, when the babysitter arrived, she found the door locked, and before she could get a workman to open the door, the poet was dead.

The adolescent may not have a clear idea whether he or she really intends to die or merely to make a gesture. But it must be emphasised that apparent suicidal attempts are always to be taken seriously, whatever the motivation for them. They are a *cry for help*—and generally a desperate one.

Why should a young person attempt suicide?
In considering this question, it is necessary to distinguish between immediate precipitating events and longer-term predisposing factors. Precipitating events may include the breakup or threatened breakup of a romance, pregnancy (real or imagined), school failure, conflicts with parents, rejection by a friend, being apprehended in a socially proscribed or delinquent act, loss of a parent or other loved person, fear of serious illness or imminent mental breakdown, and the like. On closer examination, however,

it often becomes clear that the young person's reaction to such an event is really the culmination of a series of mounting difficulties.

Adolescents who attempt suicide often have a long history of disturbed family relationships. Marital discord between parents, emotional problems in parents, parental divorce or remarriage, even abandonment, are often in the backgrounds of adolescents who attempt suicide. But even where such obvious signs of family instability may be missing, there is likely to be a *loss of communication* between parent and child. The adolescent thus feels unable to turn to them for support. Adolescents may try to compensate for this by seeking emotional support from other people, and if these also turn out to be no help the consequence can be serious. A sense of isolation may lead the adolescent to feel that suicide is all that is left to do.

Preventing adolescent suicides

It is a dangerous myth that a person who talks about committing suicide will not do so. Any talk of suicide should always be treated as potentially serious. But predicting actual risk is not easy.

Some of the signs to watch for are shown in the accompanying box. The most important thing to remember is to trust your own judgment and seek help if you think a friend or relative is potentially suicidal. Don't worry about breaking a confidence if someone reveals suicidal plans to you. You may have to betray a secret in order to save a life.[5]

If you are a parent, encourage the young person to talk to you. Don't give false reassurances that 'everything will be all right' and don't tell the young person 'to cheer up and snap out of it'. Listen and sympathise with what the boy or girl says. Show him or her that you care and want to help. And seek professional assistance promptly.

Counselling—both of parents and *child— is essential in cases of threatened or attempted suicide.*

Clues to suicidal risk in adolescents

1. A persistently depressed or despairing mood.
2. Eating and sleeping disturbances.
3. Declining school performance.
4. Gradual social withdrawal and increasing isolation from others.
5. Breakdown in communication with parents or other important people in the young person's life.
6. A history of previous suicidal attempts or involvement in accidents.
7. Seemingly, reckless, self-destructive, and uncharacteristic behaviour, such as serious drug or alcohol use, reckless driving.
8. Statements such as 'I wish I were dead' or 'What is there to live for?'
9. Inquiries about the lethal properties of drugs, poisons, or weapons.
10. Unusually stressful events in a young person's life, such as school failure, breakup of a love affair, loss of a loved one.

Apparently morbid self-dramatisations should not be ignored.

Eating problems

Early adolescence is a period of rapid physical and physiological change, and it is not surprising that after the onset of puberty many adolescents go through a brief period of weight fluctuations. Once their physical growth has stabilised, most young people are able to regulate their weight through adjustments in their diet. But some are unable to do this. They either eat too little or too much, or constantly shift back and forth between overeating and 'crash diets'.

Eating too little

Our society, in contrast to some others, places a great emphasis on being slim. Many adolescents, particularly those with a naturally large body structure, may eat less than good health requires in an effort to look more like some currently admired model of attractiveness such as a film or television star. The result, though hardly desirable, generally gives no real cause for parental anxiety.

There is, however, a condition of severe undereating known as *anorexia nervosa*, in which adolescents, mostly girls, undereat for so long that they become severely malnourished and their very survival may be threatened. Anorexia often begins with what appears to be a sensible diet to get rid of a few extra pounds,

Indulgent adults may say, 'It's his glands.' But the commonest cause of obesity is plain overeating.

but once the girl reaches an ideal or even a slightly underweight level, she does not, indeed cannot, stop dieting. Anorexia is a particularly puzzling condition because the adolescent has such a distorted perception of her bodily image: many anorexic girls who, to neutral observers, are nothing but skin and bone continue to express worries about putting on too much weight.

There is much we still do not know about this condition. While it is still relatively rare, it seems to be increasing in frequency. Biological factors (possibly an impairment of the functioning of the anterior pituitary gland at the base of the brain) may play some role, but psychological factors appear to be of primary importance. Parents are often surprised by the onset of anorexia because their child has always seemed so 'normal'. As children, anorexic adolescents typically seemed almost 'too good'—quiet, obedient, always dependable, eager to please. Most have been good students.

When one looks closely, however, the picture is not as bright. At least unconsciously, most anorexic young people feel that they have been exploited and prevented from leading their own lives, and that they have not been able to form a strong identity of their own. They typically lack a clear sense of emerging selfhood, despite prolonged struggles to be 'perfect' in the eyes of others. Perhaps in reaction, they are likely to display an obsessional need to be in control of every aspect of life, particularly control over their own bodies. They may also feel incapable of meeting the demands of sexual maturity. Severe undereating, which may interrupt normal menstruation or delay the menarche, sometimes for years, and make secondary sex characteristics less prominent, may appear a way of delaying or avoiding growing up. The menarche is related quite closely to body weight, and there may be some unconscious recognition of the body's approach to this critical weight.

Studies of the parents of female anorexic adolescents show that the parents have frequently exerted such firm control and regulation during childhood that the girl herself has had difficulty in establishing a sense of identity and lacks confidence in her ability to make decisions for herself. These parents are also likely to have encouraged their children to become perfectionists and over-achievers.

The treatment of anorexia may initially require carefully planned hospital treatment. But if long-term progress is to be made and relapses avoided, psychological treatment, not only of the adolescent but of parents as well, is essential.

Eating too much
Most obese adolescents become so through overeating. A few owe their large size to genetic or constitutional factors, and others may develop a physical predisposition to overweight as a result of overfeeding by parents during the early months of life. Infants are born with a certain number of fat cells, and overfeeding during infancy can result in a permanent increase in the number

and size of these cells, making normal weight difficult to achieve. A fat baby is not necessarily a healthy—or even a happy—baby.

The psychological reasons for overeating to obesity are many and various—feelings of emptiness or loneliness; anxiety about being taken care of; feelings of 'smallness' or inadequacy. It may be seen as a way of avoiding pressures for social or sexual relationships, or even just of getting out of physical exertion. In our weight-conscious society being fat excludes one from all sorts of things: obesity is as good as a chastity belt. Many obese adolescents lack a sense of independence, and feel incapable of controlling their own lives, or even their own bodies.[6] They often seem to be unsure of their own bodily urges, including hunger. The average adolescent will eat when hungry and avoid eating when full, even if food is present. This is not typically true of the obese, who tend to eat if food is present, regardless of their real need.

Helping an adolescent to lose weight needs parental support and understanding as well as a sensible diet. It will not do to nag or deride. Where significant psychological problems seem to play a part in obesity, an attempt must be made—if necessary with professional help—to determine the source of the problem.

Delinquency

Police, crowds, racial tension—and adolescents: an explosive mixture.

More than 2,000 years ago, an Egyptian priest carved on a stone, 'Our Earth is degenerate. Children no longer obey their parents.' Delinquency is no new problem. Today it includes not only the more serious offences such as burglary, assault, and robbery but also 'status offences'—acts such as curfew violation (in the USA), truancy, running away, sexual activity, or 'incorrigibility', which would not constitute violations of the law if committed by an adult.

Nevertheless, current rates of delinquency *are* cause for serious concern in many Western countries, including the United States, where the incidence of recorded delinquency has increased rapidly since 1960 with an even sharper rise in the rate for serious offences and for delinquency among girls.

What causes delinquency?

Delinquency is both a psychological and a sociological problem. The incidence is higher in socially disorganised, economically deprived areas, such as the urban ghettos of large cities. In such settings, delinquency is often an approved tradition, and delinquent gangs are common. Nevertheless, many young people from such backgrounds do *not* become delinquent—and conversely, increasingly numbers of adolescents from affluent suburban areas are becoming involved in delinquent acts.

What distinguishes the young person who becomes delinquent from one who does not, even when they share a common background?

Repressed anger and resentment in adolescence commonly vent themselves in irrational violence.

Research studies indicate that there are general differences in personality between the average delinquent and non-delinquent. Delinquents tend to be more angry and defiant, suspicious of authority, resentful, impulsive, and lacking in self-control. They also appear to have lower self-esteem and more feelings of

There is no law to say you have to be delinquent because of your background.

personal inadequacy, and emotional and social rejection. Despite their frequent outward bravado, underneath the surface, such delinquents tend to have a low opinion of themselves.

Parent-child relationships of delinquents

Although influences such as peer group pressure and a generally adverse social environment obviously play a part in delinquency, the role of parents appears crucial. With remarkable consistency, research studies indicate that 'The early disciplinary techniques to which delinquents have been subjected are likely to be lax, erratic, or overly strict, and to involve physical punishment, rather than reasoning with the child about misconduct.'[7] Among delinquents, relations between parent and child are likely to be characterised by mutual hostility, lack of family cohesiveness, and parental rejection, indifference, dissension, or apathy.

Fathers of delinquents are likely to be rated by independent observers as cruel, neglecting, and inclined to ridicule their children (particularly sons). They are less likely to be rated as warm and affectionate. In turn, their delinquent young, especially sons, are likely to have few close ties with their fathers and to consider them wholly unacceptable as models for their conduct. Mothers of delinquents are more likely to be rated as careless or inadequate in child supervision, and as hostile or indifferent rather than loving and responsible. Many delinquents also come from broken homes.

What can parents do?

In the first place, parents need to keep the problem in perspective. Delinquent behaviour should never be ignored; but many young people who become involved in *minor* delinquent acts go on to become perfectly normal, responsible adults. Sneaking into a movie without paying, 'borrowing' a peer's property, playing truant from school, even minor shoplifting are not 'crimes' comparable with burglary and mugging.

Serious and honest discussion between parent and child, conducted in a calm but realistic atmosphere, can often be helpful, especially if the basic relationship between them is one of mutual trust, affection and respect. When such communication is not possible, when it appears that emotional disturbance is playing an important part in the delinquent behaviour, or when the offence is a serious one, professional assistance should be sought.

As noted in Chapter 4, the *authoritative* parent—one who genuinely cares about the adolescent and encourages the development of independence and self-reliance, but who also sets standards of responsible, appropriate behaviour—is less likely to have a delinquent son or daughter than the parent who is authoritarian, rejecting, overly permissive, or neglectful.

10 Looking to the future

If parents are asked what they want most in life for their children, the answer is likely to be 'happiness'. But where does happiness lie, and how can we help our young people to achieve it? By helping them to become financially secure? By looking out for their health? By protecting them from tragedy and misfortune? We can certainly make efforts in these directions, but in this unpredictable world, we cannot be confident of more than temporary success. Many of the challenges that young people will eventually have to meet and the adaptations they will have to make are impossible to predict: one need only look at last year's 'expert' estimates of what today's world would be like to see the truth of this. But if parents cannot provide their children with a blueprint for the future, or prescribe how they should lead their lives, what can they do?

If we look unsparingly at reality, it seems to me that the best insurance we can work toward for our children is the development of a clear and confident sense of their own identity and a commitment to some system of basic values. Without this, human existence can have little real meaning or purpose. Life brings many crises and disappointments to all of us. But emotionally mature young people—those who are able to achieve a workable integration of their own needs and desires, their conscience and ideals, and the demands of the real world—will be far better prepared to cope with the inevitable 'slings and arrows of outrageous fortune' than the immature, the rigid and inflexible, the rootless and self-indulgent, or the neurotic.

Being 'mentally healthy' does not mean being able to go through life without conflict. No one can avoid conflicts between his or her needs, goals and desires and the demands of reality, or between opposing internal needs—in any case, a reasonable amount of conflict often serves as an impetus to further personal growth and development. What parents can—and should—do is to help their children to learn to tolerate a reasonable amount of conflict and frustration, and to deal with it effectively, to be realistic and moderate in needs and fears.

In tune with
her world: the
full-blooded joy
of adolescence.

Sigmund Freud was once asked what he meant by emotional maturity. '*Lieben und arbeiten*', he replied—the capacity to love and to work. By genuinely loving our children (which certainly does not preclude moments of acute frustration and irritation), by valuing and respecting them as people, by enjoying their company, by being worthy of their trust, we can help them to become capable, in their turn, of loving and trusting others.

By encouraging sons and daughters to become independent, competent, self-reliant and responsible, we can help them, in Freud's words 'to work'—that is, to be prepared to meet the challenges of changing vocational demands and responsible citizenship. As we have seen, this is best accomplished by 'authoritative' or 'democratic' parenting, not by authoritarian *or* by *laissez faire*, overly permissive child rearing—and certainly not by neglect or indifference.

But parents alone should not, in a modern society, be expected to do the whole job. Children need adequate nutrition and health care; they need to grow up in decent surroundings; they need to be around peers and adults who can provide models of successful, socially responsible behaviour. And they need a good education, which can challenge and develop their native abilities, and prepare them for rewarding careers and responsible citizenship. Finally, when they enter young adulthood, they need to find jobs to be filled, and they need to be accepted as fully-fledged members of society.

Something to do, and someone to do it with— but happiness can depend on having enough to buy a bicycle.

Do we really care?

For all too many of our young people, these needs are being poorly met, when they are met at all. Unless Western society begins to demonstrate a greater sense of responsibility to its young people—not just the socially, economically, or ethnically favoured, but *all* its children—we will continue to see rising rates of personal failure and tragedy, of delinquency, suicide, psychiatric problems and alienation.

Perhaps more than at any time in history, we loudly proclaim our devotion to the welfare of children and adolescents. But to date we have done far too little to put our pious protestations into practice. Too many children in most countries still grow to nominal adulthood in poverty—malnourished, poorly housed and clothed, lacking in adequate health care and exposed to crime, violence and exploitation. Too many young people emerge from our schools (when they have not already dropped out in frustration) poorly prepared for gainful employment or even the demands of daily living.

Lacking facilities or guidance, what else is there to do but loaf around waiting for something exciting to happen?

The situation is worst for those growing up in urban or rural slums. Here overburdened, discouraged teachers with inadequate resources and community support often have difficulty even in maintaining a semblance of discipline and order in the classroom, let alone providing an education relevant to the needs of their students. And even middle class schools often provide little cause for unbridled enthusiasm. Charles Silberman, in a nationwide survey of secondary education in the United States, found a

Exercise, order and discipline—but is it 'training for docility'?

Exercise, underlying order and self-expression.

tendency in many middle class schools to concentrate on what he calls 'education for docility'.[1] This means an over-emphasis on order, discipline, and conformity at the expense of self-expression, intellectual curiosity, creativity, and the development of humane, sensitive human beings concerned with values, capable of self-reliance and independent judgment, and able and willing to learn for themselves.

Other countries will vary in their conformity to these findings according to such factors as attitudes to social class, the split between private and state-provided education, emphasis on public achievement and so on. But there is no doubt that *in general* in the Western world, education is designed to shape rather than to encourage growth. There is much talk about the need for self-direction; but '[many] schools discourage students from developing the capacity to learn by and for themselves; they make it impossible for a youngster to take responsibility for his own education, for they are structured in such a way as to make students totally dependent upon the teachers. Whatever rhetoric they may subscribe to, most schools in practice define education as something teachers do to or for students, not something students do to and for themselves, with a teacher's assistance.'[2]

This situation is likely to be most pronounced at the junior high school levels. Adolescents are harder to 'control' than younger children, and secondary schools are thus likely to be even more authoritarian and repressive then elementary schools. 'The values they transmit are the values of docility, passivity, conformity and lack of trust.'[3] This is especially ironic because it is at this time that cognitive changes open wider intellectual and cultural horizons than the younger child is capable of envisaging.

Obviously not all schools fit these dismal patterns. Even in some urban ghettos, there are schools that are spectacularly successful. One such school is in a rundown section of New York City, where adolescent girls, who had previously been rejected as incapable or unmanageable by other city schools, not only proved able to stay in school, but to develop a sense of pride in themselves and their school, and to improve their educational skills spectacularly. Here, often for the first time, many of the parents who had long treated the schools with suspicion or indifference as just another arm of an exploitative 'establishment' became enthusiastic and involved supporters of this particular school's efforts.

How was this 'miracle' achieved? Researchers studying this and other successful educational efforts found several essential ingredients. The atmosphere is a good bit warmer and more supportive than in most schools. Disruptive behaviour is handled more positively, and there is a conviction that 'disadvantaged' children can learn. Principals and teachers in these schools hold *themselves* accountable if their students fail, and innovative, imaginative, pupil-centred approaches to the development of academic skills are flexibly employed. Far more such schools—and teachers—are badly needed.

Don't call us, we'll call you
Once they have left school, or even college, too many young people find our economic system ill-prepared to provide a meaningful place—or sometimes even any place—for them. In

the United States, for example, from 1947 to 1965, youth employment averaged 2·5 times higher than total unemployment, even though both fluctuated widely; from 1965 to the present, youth unemployment has been more than three times higher. Recently, among black teenagers, nationwide unemployment *among those seeking work* reached an incredible 40 per cent. Somewhat similar problems exist in other countries, even among the college-educated. In Italy, for example, the number of university-educated young people far exceeds the demand for them, even in professions such as law and architecture.

The problem is greatest, however, for the average youth. Young, lacking specific vocational skills and experience, they find it difficult or impossible to enter an already crowded marketplace. Employers often prefer to wait until they are 'more useful'. But how are they to gain the experiences that will make them more useful?

In earlier, simpler times, young people could learn vocational skills largely by following in a parent's footsteps, or through apprenticeships. In our increasingly age-segregated technological society, however, young people are seldom given such opportunities for interaction with working adults, presumably because 'it just isn't practical'.

This need not be the case. In an interesting and imaginative social experiment in the city of Chicago, two groups of 12-year-old boys and girls, one from a slum area and the other from a predominantly middle class area, spent six to seven hours a day for three days in the various departments of a newspaper, ranging from the city room to the composing room and the advertising department, 'not just observing but participating actively in the department's work'. Despite the workers' initial misgivings, both adults and young people found the experience rewarding. One worker later commented, with some amazement, that the boy assigned to him knew more about the nature of his work, and its demands and pressures, than his own adolescent son![4]

Obviously, adolescents entering the world of work need adequate protection and safeguards. This was, of course, the original purpose of our child labour laws; but there is reason to believe it has been carried too far in contemporary society and has contributed to the 'alienation' of young people and their alleged 'incapacity' to deal constructively with personal and social problems. The evidence indicates that children acquire the capacity to cope with difficult situations when they have an opportunity to take on consequential responsibilities in relation to others and are held accountable for them.

It is clear that the problem of planning for and gaining entrance to a vocation is one of the critical developmental tasks of adolescence. But if all our young people are to accomplish this task successfully, far more flexibility and a greater sense of commitment by society is necessary. The problem of finding appropriate employment—even, in some cases, any employment at all—for young people is not a simple one. It is likely to become even more difficult in the future as our entire society grows more complex, more specialised, more technologically oriented, and more subject to the effects of forces beyond our immediate control. But unless the problem can be resolved, unless some better match can be found between vocational opportunities and the needs, educational preparation, talents, skills, and values of young people, society and its youth will be in serious trouble.

Epilogue

Growing up in today's world is not easy, either for adolescents themselves or for their parents. Adolescents still have the traditional need to adjust to a self that is rapidly changing physically, sexually, and intellectually, and to societal demands

*She is turning
her back on
childish pleasures:
he looks to the future
with an eye
to possibilities.*

for greater independence and self-reliance. Parents still have to come to terms with their own 'mid-life crises'. They also have to accept the fact that the relationship between parent and child must inevitably change in the direction of greater independence of thought and action for the young person.

In addition, however, both parents and their young are faced today with a rapidly changing world. It is one in which values and patterns of social behaviour are in flux, technological progress is accelerating, and new political, social, and environmental problems are emerging.

If I were to stress one single bit of advice for parents and their adolescent young as they struggle with all of these changes, it would be the need to keep the lines of communication between them open. When adults and adolescents were asked in a recent poll to cite any complaints they had about 'the other generation', adults mentioned a 'lack of dialogue with their elders' among their strictures on adolescents; and adolescents, in turn, complained that 'they won't listen to us'. Despite some popular notions to the contrary, the fact is that adolescents still need their parents' love, guidance, and active concern. By the same token, parents need their children, both for the greater meaning these young people can lend to their lives, and for the real contribution they can make to their parents' own continuing development and their flexibility in coping with inevitable change.[5]

References

1   A time for becoming

1. Aristotle, *Ethica Nicomachea* (trans. W. D. Ross). In R. McKeon (Ed.), *The Basic Works of Aristotle.* N Y: Random House, 1941.
2. Conrad, J. *Youth: A Narrative and Two Other Stories.* Edinburgh and London: Blackwood, 1902.
3. Butler, S. *The Way of All Flesh.* N Y: Dutton, 1910.
4. Mead, *Growing Up in New Guinea.* N Y: Mentor Books, 1953.
5. Hudson, W. H. *Far Away and Long Ago.* N Y: Dutton, 1918, pp. 292–295.
6. Erikson, E. H. *Identity: Youth and Crisis.* N Y: Norton, 1968.
7. Lynd, H. *On Shame and the Search for Identity.* N Y: Science Editions, 1966, pp. 228–229.
8. Spence, J. *Masculinity and Femininity: Their Psychological Dimensions, Correlates, and Antecedents.* Austin and London: University of Texas Press, 1978.

2   Growing up: the body

1. Money, J., & Ehrhardt, A. A. *Man and Woman, Boy and Girl: The Differentiation and Dimorphism of Gender Identity from Conception to Maturity.* Baltimore: Johns Hopkins University Press, 1972.
2. Tanner, J. M. Physical Growth. In P. H. Mussen (Ed.), *Carmichael's Manual of Child Psychology* (Vol. 2). N Y: Wiley, 1970 (3rd ed.), p. 94.
3. Ruble, D. N., & Brooks, J. Attitudes About Menstruation. Paper presented at the Biennial Meeting of the Society for Research in Child Development. New Orleans, March 1977.
4. Pomeroy, W. B. *Girls and Sex.* N Y: Delacorte Press, 1969, p. 47.
5. Stone, L. J. & Church, J. *Childhood and Adolescence: A Psychology of the Growing Person.* N Y: Random House, 1968, pp. 475–476.
6. Jones, M. C. The Later Careers of Boys who were Early or Late Maturing. *Child Development,* 1957, *28,* 113–128.
7. Mussen, P. H., & Jones, M. C. Self-Conceptions, Motivations, and Interpersonal Attitudes of Late and Early Maturing Boys. *Child Development,* 1957, *28,* 243–256.
8. Faust, M. S. Developmental Maturity as a Determinant in Prestige of Adolescent Girls. *Child Development,* 1960, *31,* 173–184.

3   Mental growth

1. Maccoby, E. E., & Jacklin, C. N. *The Psychology of Sex Differences.* Stanford, Calif.: Stanford University Press, 1974.
2. Flavell, J. H. *The Developmental Psychology of Jean Piaget.* N Y: Van Nostrand, 1963.
3. Conger, J. J. *Adolescence and Youth: Psychological Development in a Changing World* (2nd ed.). N Y: Harper & Row, 1977.
4. Elkind, D. Cognitive Development in Adolescence. In J. F. Adams (Ed.), *Understanding Adolescence.* Boston: Allyn & Bacon, 1968, p. 152.
5. Osterrieth, P. A. Adolescence: Some Psychological Aspects. In G. Caplan & S. Lebovici (Eds.). *Adolescence: Psychosocial Perspectives.* N Y: Basic Books, 1969, p. 15.

6. Elkind, D. Egocentrism in Adolescence. *Child Development*, 1967, *38*, 1025–1034.

4 Adolescents and their parents

1. Douvan, E., & Adelson, J. *The Adolescent Experience.* N Y: Wiley, 1966, p. 351.
2. Storr, C. *Growing Up: A Practical Guide to Adolescence for Parents and Children.* London: Arrow Books, 1975.
3. Ford, C. S. Some Primitive Societies. In G. H. Seward & R. C. Williamson (Eds.). *Sex Roles in Changing Society.* N Y: Random House, 1970, p. 178.
4. Yankelovich, D. *Generations Apart.* N Y: Columbia Broadcasting System, 1969.
5. Yankelovich, D. *The New Morality: A Profile of American Youth in the 70s.* N Y: McGraw-Hill, 1974.
6. Conger, J. J. *Adolescence and Youth: Psychological Development in a Changing World* (2nd ed.). N Y: Harper & Row, 1977.
7. Konopka, G. *Young Girls: A Portrait of Adolescence.* Englewood Cliffs, N. J.: Prentice-Hall, 1976, p. 81.
8. Ibid, p. 65.
9. Ibid, p. 71.
10. Baumrind, D. Authoritarian vs. Authoritative Control. *Adolescence,* 1968, *3*, 255–272.
    Elder, G. H., Jr. Parental Power Legitimation and Its Effect on the Adolescent. *Sociometry,* 1963, *26*, 50–65.
11. Conger, J. J. *Adolescence: The Winds of Change* (film). N Y.: Harper & Row, 1976.

5 Adolescents and sex

1. Sorensen, R. C. *Adolescent Sexuality in Contemporary America: Personal Values and Sexual Behavior Ages 13–19.* N Y: Harry N. Abrams, 1973.
2. Ibid.
3. Ibid.
4. Conger, J. J. *Adolescence and Youth: Psychological Development in a Changing World* (2nd ed.). N Y: Harper & Row, 1977.
5. Sorensen, R. C. op. cit.
6. Luckey, E. B., & Nass, G. D. A Comparison of Sexual Attitudes and Behavior in an International Sample. *Journal of Marriage and the Family,* 1969, *31*, 364–379.
7. Sorensen, R. C. op. cit.
8. Jessor, S. L., & Jessor, R. Transition from Virginity to Nonvirginity Among Youth: A Social-Psychological Study Over Time. *Developmental Psychology,* 1975, *11*, 473–484.
9. Sorensen, R. C. op. cit.
10. Fine, L. *After All We've Done for Them.* Englewood Cliffs, N. J.: Prentice Hall, 1977.
11. Alan Guttmacher Institute (AGI). *11 Million Teenagers: What Can Be Done About the Epidemic of Adolescent Pregnancies in the United States.* N Y: Planned Parenthood Federation of America, 1976.
12. Chilman, C. S. *Social and Psychological Aspects of Adolescent Sexuality: An Analytic Overview of Research and Theory.* Milwaukee, Wisconsin: Center for Advanced Studies in Human Sciences, School of Social Welfare, University of Wisconsin, 1977.
13. Kaplan, H. S. *The New Sex Therapy: Active Treatment of Sexual Dysfunctions.* N Y: Bruner/Mazel, 1974.
14. Hunt, M. *Sexual Behavior in the 1970s.* Chicago: Playboy Press, 1975.

6   Adolescents and their peers

1. Mussen, P. H., Conger, J. J., & Kagan, J. *Child Development and Personality* (4th ed.). N Y: Harper & Row, 1974, p. 574.
2. Conger, J. J. *Adolescence and Youth: Psychological Development in a Changing World* (2nd ed.). N Y: Harper & Row, 1977.
3. Stone, L. J., & Church, J. *Childhood and Adolescence: A Psychology of the Growing Person* (3rd ed.). N Y: Random House, 1973, p. 442.
4. Jersild, A. T. *The Psychology of Adolescence* (2nd ed.). N Y: Macmillan, 1963, p. 254.
5. Konopka, G. *Young Girls: A Portrait of Adolescence.* Englewood Cliffs, N. J.: Prentice-Hall, 1976, p. 85.
6. Douvan, E., & Adelson, J. *The Adolescent Experience.* N Y: Wiley, 1966.
7. Ibid.
8. Coleman, J. C. *Relationships in Adolescence.* London: Routledge and Kegan Paul, 1975.
9. Douvan, E., & Adelson, J. op. cit.
10. Alan Guttmacher Institute. *11 Million Teenagers: What Can Be Done About the Epidemic of Adolescent Pregnancies in the United States.* N Y: Planned Parenthood Federation of America, 1976.

7   Adolescents and drugs

1. Shafer, R. P., et al. *Drug Use in America: Problem in Perspective.* Second Report of the National Commission on Marijuana and Drug Abuse. Washington, D. C.: U.S. Government Printing Office, No. 5266-00003, 1973.
2. *Alcohol and Health: New Knowledge.* Second Special Report to the U.S. Congress, National Institute on Alcohol Abuse and Alcoholism, Department of Health, Education and Welfare. Washington, D.C.: Superintendent of Documents, U.S. Government Printing Office, No. 1724–00399. June 1974 (preprint edition).
    Single, E., Kandel, D., & Faust, R. Patterns of Multiple Drug Use in High School. *Journal of Health and Social Behavior,* 1974, *15,* 344–357.
3. *Marihuana and Health.* Fifth Annual Report to Congress from the Secretary of Health, Education and Welfare. Washington, D.C.: U.S. Government Printing Office, 1975.
4. Child Study Association of America. *You, Your Child, and Drugs.* N Y: Child Study Press, 1971, p. 18.
5. Ibid., p. 24
6. Yolles, S. Statement before the Subcommittee on the Judiciary, U.S. Senate, September 17, 1969 (mimeographed), p. 24.

8   Moral growth and alienation

1. Conger, J. J. *Adolescence and Youth: Psychological Development in a Changing World* (2nd. ed.). N Y: Harper & Row, 1977.
2. Tapp, J. L., & Levine, F. J. Compliance from Kindergarten to College: A Speculative Research Note. *Journal of Youth and Adolescence,* 1972, *1,* 233–249.
3. Hoffman, M. L. Moral Development. In P. H. Mussen (Ed.), *Carmichael's Manual of Child Psychology* (Vol. 2). N Y: Wiley, 1970.
4. Ibid., p. 292.
5. Ibid., p. 285.
6. Conger, J. J. Alienation: An Overview. In B. B. Wolman (Ed.), *International Encyclopedia of Psychiatry, Psychology, Psychoanalysis, and Neurology,* Vol. I. New York: Aesculapius Publishers, 1977, pp. 430–433.

9 Psychological problems

1. Senn, M. J. E., & Solnit, A. J. *Problems in Child Behavior and Development.* Philadelphia: Lea & Febiger, 1968.
2. Weiner, I. B. *Psychological Disturbance in Adolescence.* N Y: Wiley, 1970.
3. Josselyn, I. M. *Adolescence.* N Y: Harper & Row, 1971, p. 58.
4. Ibid., p. 59.
5. Klagsburn, F. *Youth and Suicide: Too Young to Die.* N Y: Pocket Books, 1970.
6. Bruch, H. *Eating Disorders.* N Y: Basic Books, 1973.
7. Conger, J. J. *Adolescence and Youth: Psychological Development in a Changing World* (2nd ed.). N Y: Harper & Row, 1977, p. 583.

10 Looking to the future

1. Silberman, Charles E. *Crisis in the Classroom: The Remaking of American Education.* New York: Random House, 1970.
2. Ibid., p. 135.
3. Ibid., p. 324.
4. Bronfenbrenner, U. The Origins of Alienation. *Scientific American,* 1974, *231,* 53–61.
5. Conger, John J. A World They Never Knew: The Family and Social Change. *Daedalus,* Fall 1971, 1105–1138.

Index